P9-CQZ-360

THE
SHAAR
PRESS

THE JUDAICA IMPRINT
FOR THOUGHTFUL PEOPLE

Some-thing

A SHAAR PRESS PUBLICATION

to Think About

Extraordinary reflections about ordinary events

RABBI YAAKOV SALOMON, C.S.W.

© *Copyright 2005 by* Shaar Press

First edition – First impression / December 2005

ALL RIGHTS RESERVED

No part of this book may be reproduced **in any form,** *photocopy, electronic media, or otherwise without* **written** *permission from the copyright holder, except by a reviewer who wishes to quote brief passages in connection with a review written for inclusion in magazines or newspapers.*
THE RIGHTS OF THE COPYRIGHT HOLDER WILL BE STRICTLY ENFORCED.

Published by **SHAAR PRESS**
Distributed by MESORAH PUBLICATIONS, LTD.
4401 Second Avenue / Brooklyn, N.Y 11232 / (718) 921-9000 / www.artscroll.com

Distributed in Israel by SIFRIATI / A. GITLER
6 Hayarkon Street / Bnei Brak 51127

Distributed in Europe by LEHMANNS
Unit E, Viking Business Park, Rolling Mill Road / Jarrow, Tyne and Wear, NE32 3DP/ England

Distributed in Australia and New Zealand by GOLDS WORLD OF JUDAICA
3-13 William Street / Balaclava, Melbourne 3183 / Victoria Australia

Distributed in South Africa by KOLLEL BOOKSHOP
Shop 8A Norwood Hypermarket / Norwood 2196, Johannesburg, South Africa

ISBN: 1-4226-0092-0 Hard Cover

Printed in the United States of America by Noble Book Press
Custom bound by Sefercraft, Inc. / 4401 Second Avenue / Brooklyn N.Y. 11232

Table of Contents

It's All About Relationships

Searching for Spirituality

That's Just Human Nature

Setting the Table

Time, time, time...

Thank You

*H*ere's a challenge to you, the readers:

Nearly every Jewish book I read begins the "Acknowledgments" by thanking Hashem for all the wonderful good He has bestowed upon the author. It is usually accompanied by some lame attempt to "fully and accurately express" the extent of the author's appreciation to the Creator, with words that often prove to be less than adequate.

But in truth, this book, in its essence, is really being offered as one giant *Thank You* to the One Who Is All. The best way…the *only* way that gratitude can really be accurately expressed is if you, the reader, come away from these pages with *Something to Think About*, and then something to do! In my mind, if you come closer to Him by virtue of anything I have written, there will have been no greater expression of thanks possible. May my hope be fulfilled!

It was about four years ago when I received an email from Rabbi Nechemia Coopersmith. Rabbi C had, not long before, assumed the position as editor-in-chief of Aish.com — the fastest growing Jewish content website in the world. He was looking for writers and sought me out. The rest is history. Most of the collection herein is culled from those margins. The millions of visits that aish.com now boasts *each month* are living testimony to his keen eye and unyielding determination to educate and energize every living Jew.

On a personal level, Rabbi Coopersmith has enhanced my writing tenfold by his creativity, his constant encouragement, and his uncanny ability to keep lifting the bar higher and higher, and daring me to meet and surpass it. And when I didn't, he made sure to tell me about it. I wasn't always happy, but I hope he never stops. Together with Rabbi Shraga Simmons, Yitzchok Attias and an incredible staff, they have dramatically unbolted the portals of Torah to countless Jews around the globe. My association with them is an honor and my gratitude is enormous.

The highest order of Divine Providence led me to Aish Hatorah more than 16 years ago and my respect and awe for this citadel of Torah is still growing. Few parts of my life have not been deeply affected by its Dean and Founder, Rabbi Noach Weinberg *shlita,* and his outstretched arms of disciples, ideas, branches, programs, students, and love. I am forever grateful to him for having given me the opportunity to grow and to give; to teach and to toil; to learn and to understand life. Allowing me to write his book, *What the Angel Taught You* (Shaar Press), was an experience I will always cherish. May Hashem grant you many more years of vision and clarity to continue leading us on the path to Mashiach.

Truthfully, my connections with Aish would have been valuable enough just for having introduced Rabbi Yitzchok Coopersmith into my life. His unsurpassed humility will surely prevent him from believing how much he has contributed to my writing, my teaching, and my understanding of life's priorities and subtleties. Thanks for always making things so clear to me.

Isn't life wonderful when you can find a valued and true friend who is so much younger than you? I had known Reb Chaim Goldbaum for many years, but when we became *chavrusos* a short while back, I discovered a very special person and most valuable resource all in one. A bona fide *talmid chacham,* Chaim has rapidly become a constant confidant, a skilled editor and evaluator, and a great sidekick of mine. All that is written here was poured through his loving and precise filter before being mixed thoroughly and served. His passion for life, devotion to truth, and genuine caring have enriched my worlds and my words. Besides, he also laughs at all my jokes. Thank you, Chaim, for everything.

When you write for the public, you bare your soul. And you expose yourself to the erasers, highlighters, and red markers of every frustrated writer and editor at large. Fortunate is the author who surrounds himself with talented and candid critics who never fail to let him know exactly what they think while trampling ever so gingerly around his frail and rickety ego.

Besides the aforementioned individuals, a dedicated cadre of referees have, for the past years, read, re-read, commented, corrected, argued, and applauded my pennings.

Rabbi Paysach Krohn *shlita*, quickly becoming the most famous and admired Jew in the world, somehow finds a few precious moments nearly every day for me. No one knows how he does what he does. It doesn't really matter. I'm just glad for the privilege of being called his friend.

It doesn't seem to make a difference how busy Dr. Meir Wikler is. When I call, he responds — quickly, sensitively, brilliantly, and with genuine care. The list of things we share is endless; this book is just one more example. Thanks for the constant kudos and critiques. No one knows how to praise better than you do. No wonder you have eight (or nine?) amazing books to your credit.

Every time one of my children reads something of mine, I revel in his/her reaction — be it rave or roast. I consider their comfort in telling it to me straight, to be a giant testimony to our closeness and mutual respect. Kids, you are all fantastic sounding boards for me in everything I write. I mention each one of you by name and treasure your judgment and encouragement more than you can imagine. Thank you Naftali and Layala, Aharon and Rifki, Noshi and Mimi, Shmuel and Reena, Avi, Tova, Yehuda, and Chanala. I am in awe of you, your own darling children, and your remarkable achievements already, and I thank Hashem constantly that you are all mine.

How many authors can count their mother and brother in their selected literary reviewing fraternity? My dear mother שתחי', Mrs. Lea Salomon, somehow reads everything I write — with love, pride, and total objectivity. Only she could be capable of that. She finds errors and inconsistencies that polished professionals miss or disregard. Your strength, conviction, and courage is an inspiration to everyone you meet. And my parents-in-law, Rabbi and Mrs. Aron Sternberg, have similarly inspired me with their storied history of self-sacrifice for *chinuch* (education) in America.

No one takes more interest in my writing and in everything I do than Brother Izzy, my only and older sib. Together with Miriam, he acts as the perfect resonating chamber for every sentiment or construct I conjure up. And besides all of his sage counsel and discernment, he offers me the greatest gift of all — time. Thanks.

Rabbi Hillel David *shlita* continues, for over thirty-five years now, to provide me with everything I need in a Rav and a mentor. I have never left a conversation with him without clarity of purpose and unremitting care. How fortunate my family and I have been to feel such a close kinship with him and with Harav Dovid Cohen *shlita*, both of whom have guided us through all of life's joys and tribulations. My appreciation knows no limit.

I have been blessed to have had a long and rich affiliation with the *Rebbi of all of Klal Yisrael,* Rabbi Nosson Scherman *shlita*. A beacon of sagacity and self-effacement, as well as a role model, *chavrusa* and guide, Reb Nosson has once again lent his deft editing hand to my humble work. You like brevity so I won't belabor the obvious. Where would this generation be without you?

You, together with your co-visionary Rabbi Meir Zlotowitz, and a staff of talented and dedicated individuals — Reb Sheah Brander, Reb Avraham Biderman, Reb Gedalya Zlotowitz, Reb Efraim Perlowitz, Eli Krohn, Mendy Herzberg, Mrs. Judy Dick, Mrs. Mindy Stern, and Chaya Perel Teichman to name a few — all share in whatever impact this book makes. Please accept my thanks and gratitude.

It's hard to believe that over 20 years have passed since I re-enrolled in Yeshiva Torah Vodaath's *Kollel*. The roshei yeshivah, *mashgichim*, and *avreichim* have embraced me with open arms and endowed me with Torah, *hashkafah* (philosophy), and a sterling *derech hachaim* (way of life). Rabbis Yisroel Reisman, Label Wulliger, Heshy Wolf, Moshe Lamm, Moshe Yehuda Szwerin, Sholom Smith, Yoni Levinson, and Zev Smith in particular, have extended themselves in their continuing charade of treating me like a peer instead of a *talmid*. It is a kind conspiracy. I thank them and still enjoy it.

Special mention must be made of my *yedid neeman* (true friend), Rabbi Yerachmiel Milstein. Reb Yerachmiel has helped tens of thousands of assimilated and disenfranchised Jews find their way back to a life of meaning and contentment. No amount of recognition he receives will ever be commensurate with the credit he is due. All I do is watch him and learn. Hopefully, some of his devotion will rub off on me. *Chazak veematz* (Be strong).

Rabbi Yonah and Miriam Weinrib, *ovdei Hashem* (servants of G-d) of the highest order, and their most extraordinary children, continue to be paragons of virtue and selflessness. Everyone they touch is uplifted by their embodiment of *kedushah* (spirituality). May Hashem grant us continuing opportunities to collaborate in bringing Hashem's glory to greater intensity and magnitude.

My other *chavrusos* (study partners), Dr. Chaim Weiss and Shmuel Silberberg, always stimulate my learning, my thinking, and my *yiras Shamayim* (fear of G-d). Our learning is something I cherish. Thank you both.

Dr. David Lieberman, noted author and psychologist, has offered many valuable suggestions in my publishing efforts. More than that, his friendship, along with that of his brother Adam, is very special to me. Both of you do not realize how much your personal development and love mean to me. Thanks.

Some of the articles you are about to read first appeared in "The Jewish Observer" or in "American Jewish Spirit." Editors Rabbis Nisson Wolpin and Dovid Goldman, respectively, are the forces behind these distinguished periodicals and I am grateful for their giving me the opportunity to share my musings on their pages.

Some people will expect to see their names here. These people do not. Without their knowledge, they have raised and deepened my writing scope and skills just by virtue of their own superior writing. They are: Rabbis Yonason Rosenblum, Avi Shafran, Chaim Dovid Zwiebel; Mrs. Sara Yocheved Rigler, Wendy Shalit, and Sarah Shapiro. They represent the very best among us by always raising the standards to which we must measure up. Thank you.

I must also salute the creativity of Lawrence Stroll of Atlanta, Georgia who kindly crafted the fine subtitle of this book: *Extraordinary Reflections About Ordinary Events.* Good job!

I have saved my final acknowledgment for the most important one. My dear wife, Temmy, is reading this with discomfort — eschewing the limelight, as always. But in truth, it is I who should be uncomfortable in taking credit and honor that is really due her. No, she doesn't actually serve as my ghost writer, but so much of my thinking, insight, inspiration, and expressions come directly from her caring soul. Her duties as our *akeres habayis* (foundation of the home) are assumed with ultimate devotion and exceptional skill. Her voice, brimming with loyalty and gentility, can be found on nearly every page. Hashem has blessed me in abundance. Thanks for keeping me on track and for so much patience and understanding.

Finally, a word to my readers. If you ever meet a writer who claims he doesn't need feedback, run. Readers' feedback — positive and negative and everything in between — is the fuel that powers the writing engine. Those of you who have kindly expended the energy to offer comments these last years — in writing, thru emails, or personally — should know how much your responses have meant to me. Sometimes it stings and sometimes it enchants. But it is always greatly appreciated.

Enjoy the ride and the read.

I'd love to hear from you at YSalomon@aish.com

Yaakov Salomon

Kislev 5766 – December 2005

Welcome

*M*y favorite color is bright orange. But my favorite *pants* color is gray.

I like my music a bit louder than most do. But my favorite *pants* color is gray.

The part in my hair is, oddly, on the right side of my head. But my favorite *pants* color is still gray...and will probably always be gray.

I have always looked at my life as a curious blend of extremes and nonconformance on the one hand, and moderation and temperance on the other. This is easily explained. You see, I grew up on the Upper West Side of Manhattan — the hotbed of avant-garde living, in the turbulent and unpredictable 60's, but I have spent the last 30 plus years in Flatbush — home of the humdrum life of the everyday *galus* Jew.

I have studied in *modern* yeshivos, very *right wing* yeshivos, and in universities of the highest caliber. I read publications that span the spectrum of ideologies, opinions and persuasions. But more than anything else, my values, perceptions and life-decisions are scalloped by my teachers and my close friends, of which I have been blessed with many.

With apologies to the esteemed periodical, I have long considered myself a *Jewish Observer*. Of course, trying to distill clarity from murk, direction from disarray, and teachings from upheaval in today's complex and tangled world is no easy task. And yet, that is really the imperative for all of us as we attempt to live lives that are more meaningful, more purposeful, and more worthy of Mashiach's imminent arrival.

The legacy that has been most deeply instilled in me can best be described by the words: *"B'chol derachecha da'eihu, v'hu yiyasher orchosecha* — Know G-d in all your ways and He will smooth your paths" (*Proverbs* 3:6). the promise of King Solomon is that seeing the imprint of the A-mighty in every nuance of life is not only exhilarating — it is also a highly effective strategy for coping with life's inescapable adversities. Once you focus on the spiritual component of all that is experiential, no situation seems nearly as puzzling or overwhelming.

And so, I have embarked on a campaign to look at events with which we all are familiar, with an eye slanted heavenward. Embracing the doctrine of the Ramban (Nachmanides) that no leaf falls in the forest without the full will and intent of the Creator, I find myself increasingly focused on attempting to see the Master and extrapolating His message, even in mundane situations. For, in truth, God and the ordinary may just be the ultimate oxymoron.

How we choose to perceive the world around us is indeed, just that — a choice. And it is, arguably, one of the most crucial choices we will ever make. I have often said that when we observe the phenomena that fill our day we can either see the titles or we can see the Author. When we choose the former and see only the "What," instead of the "How, Who, When, and Why," we rob ourselves of countless opportunities to connect our souls to the *Tzelem Elokim* (Divine image) within us that longs for unification and alliance.

But when we choose the latter and we see the Author Himself, we become engaged in a state of constant fusion with the sublime. That process is exhilarating. The joy that emanates from being able to live in that sacred space has no equal on this planet. It is the raw material that enables us to fulfill the mitzvah (commandment) of *v'halachta bidrachav* (and you shall walk in His ways; *Deuteronomy* 28:9) to its fullest capacity.

In the pages that follow, you will be invited to immerse yourself in that charge. Much of what I have noticed these past few years has been instrumental in my own personal and very much ongoing expedition. And putting my observations into the written word has played no small part in that journey. But I do not expect (and nor should you) that any single cursory reading — or two or three or ten readings, for that matter — of any particular rendering ahead will automatically catapult you into a Holy swath. Heaven knows (all too well) that it takes more than a few pithy musings, however poignant, amusing, and insightful they might try to be, to transport you to a more hallowed place.

But my hope is that you will dip into my well and dwell for a spell. Splash around for a while, and perhaps the waters will begin to become familiar to you...safe and maybe even refreshing. "I recognize this place," you'll muse, "I just never fully understood the potential and profundity that permeate the experience here." But make no mistake; G-d is forever speaking to us — in more ways than we will ever be able to imagine.

I'm just trying to adjust the antenna.

Enjoy.

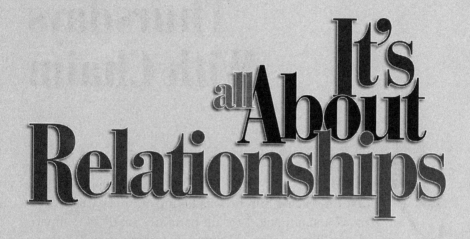

It's all About Relationships

Thursdays With Chaim

The first time I saw him he was taking out his garbage.

It was a small bag, I recall; certainly small in comparison with my Olympic size, industrial strength parcel, bulging and leaking and tearing at the seams. Calling them *Glad* bags was clearly a cruel joke or an oxymoron, I thought.

Neither of us said, *"Good morning."* I guess we each thought the other one would. We both just sort of nodded politely and re-entered our respective neighboring homes. I was busy.

Having just moved in, I spent much of my first couple of weeks repeating the garbage removal scene — mostly boxes, pizza and otherwise — but I rarely caught more than a fleeting glimpse of him. I concluded that he must be the reclusive type, but truthfully, I hardly gave it much thought at all. I was busy, you know.

Years passed. The kids grew up, new kids were born, and the garbage was setting new records. Every once in a while I'd see Chaim (really Hyman, but everyone called him Chaim) trimming his hedges (I knew his name because occasionally I received his mail by mistake), but he was "older," probably retired, I mused, and we seemed to have nothing at all in common. By this time we had graduated to the *"Good morning"* and *"Snow coming"* stages of communication, but that was pretty much it. And I can't really say that our non-relationship bothered me very much. I had plenty of friends on the block and my family, religion, and career dominated my every waking moment. You guessed it — I was busy.

I don't remember when things changed. It may have been after I invited him to one of my children's weddings. Or it may have been after we stood outside one day discussing the parking regulations on our block. I'm not sure. But something did change. He wasn't reclusive — he was shy, I discovered, almost timid, and we did have things in common, after all, like a really dry sense of humor. Out of nowhere, Chaim would say the funniest and most unexpected things with a face as straight as a cookie sheet and I would double-over and roar out loud. And every time I did that, the corners of his mouth would lift ever so slightly, as if to say, *"Finally, someone understands me."*

One year, after refusing dozens of invitations to join our family at our Shabbos table, he stunned me with his acceptance to "stop in" to our *succah* — *"just to take a look."* Exceedingly bashful, he was in and out in about 4 minutes, and spent more time apologizing about "intruding" than he did shaking my *lulav* and *esrog* awkwardly. Chaim was born and bred in Brooklyn, but received very little Jewish education or exposure in his formative years. As such, his familiarity with law and tradition was quite minimal.

Early one morning, not long after that, I nearly tripped over a small brown paper bag on my doorstep. It was in the pre-9/11 era, so I simply bent down and opened it. Inside were three small tomatoes. I searched for a note — in the bag and on it. There wasn't any. It was several days later when Chaim, his face redder than the tomatoes, inquired how I liked his little home-grown gift.

> *"I'm not sure how ripe they were and...er...and...usually they're a little more firm,"* he excused, in typical self-deprecating Chaim style.
>
> *"Oh, they were great,"* I reassured. *"Thanks."*

The poets were right. A tree really did grow in Brooklyn. And on it, a relationship had begun to blossom.

But relationships, we know, are never static. Like any good tomato, if they are not watered and nurtured they can falter and wilt and even die. And so, I decided to ask Chaim to become my Torah study partner. Mindful of his social reticence and near-total inability to take anything from anybody, I knew this was not going to be easy.

But I really thought we both had so much to gain by it, so I began planning my approach.

I was certain that the timing and wording of the invitation were crucial and that I also needed a potent and convincing argument to counter his certain dismissal of this unexpected and perhaps outlandish proposal. And it took many weeks of mental scripting and rehearsal until the day finally arrived. We were standing outside, of course, (he had never, ever trespassed my hallowed threshold...nor I, his) chatting about nothing, when I realized the time was *"Now!"*

I remember feeling foolish as I pondered my exaggerated angst. And so, I plowed ahead.

> *"I was thinking, Chaim. What do you say...you and I...study Torah together — maybe once a week, for an hour or so?"*

I had done it. I felt the mysterious anxiety wash away in an instant as I braced for his reaction. Predictably, it was totally unpredictable.

> *"Of course! That's a wonderful idea," he said. "When shall we start?"*

Well, you could have knocked me over with a *Glad* bag.

> *"When shall we start?" I bumbled.*

Now there was something I hadn't prepared for.

> *"Um...well...I suppose...er...we could start...eh...Thursday."*

Noon Thursday came and sure enough the doorbell rang. His steps were very short and his gait, saturated with trepidation. I had never seen him wearing a yarmulke before, except that one time in my *succah*, but somehow, amid all the discomfort, he looked proud.

I directed him to my dining-room table and invited him to sit and relax for a moment while I fetched some drinks for us. When I returned, seltzer and cups in hand, he was still standing — erect, as if he were awaiting roll call at Fort Dix.

> *"Because I'm waiting for you to sit first," he explained matter of factly.*

Given his penchant for formality, I suppose I should not have been surprised that he also declined the seltzer.

We divided our hour in half — studying, in English, the laws of proper speech by the Chofetz Chaim (early 20th century sage and scholar) and *Sefer HaTodaah* (The Book of Our Heritage) by Eliyahu Kitov. His background was limited, but his grasp, curiosity, and inquisitiveness were off the charts. He commented on every passage we read, and asked questions that appeared to have been lying dormant for 50 years or more. Sixty minutes seemed like 15.

Chaim rose to leave at a minute before 1 o'clock, announcing that his time was up.

"Thank you," he recited. *"It was very nice."*

I was surprised that he didn't salute me as he marched out, closing the door behind him. I quickly reopened it.

"Chaim," I called out, *"same time next week?"*

He seemed genuinely startled by the proposition.

"Oh...are you sure you're not too busy? I mean...er...you don't have to do this if you don't want to. You probably have your own studying to do and who knows what else, you certainly don't need me to..."
"I'll see you next week," I interrupted.

Next Thursday noon arrived, bringing Chaim with it. And so went the next Thursday, and the next, and every week thereafter. The menu hardly changed. The syllabus shifted as we completed various texts through the years (he even brought an old book on parables of the Dubno Maggid that we learned from), but he had to be forced to sit down before I did and the seltzer never did wet his lonely glass.

I marveled at Chaim's insight into complex principles. I often imagined that had he studied Torah when he was younger he might have scaled great scholastic heights. And those questions he asked, never-ending, revealed the incredible sensitivity that belied his reserved and proud manner. His obsession with fairness — to every single Jew, gentile, man, woman and child, animal and plant, and even to objects that were inanimate (*"they're all G-d's creations, aren't they?"*) — became a constant theme that permeated our weekly, hourly journey into some of life's most beautiful places.

Sometimes our trip included rest stops, where we ventured, ever so gingerly, into forbidden personal waters — childhood memories, minor medical concerns, and questions of faith. Those detours were brief, however, as Chaim preferred not to stray into regions where the waves were choppy and unpredictable. As we became closer, I kidded with him about it and every so often those mouth corners of his would leap, not curl, and his hearty laugh would fill the dining room. I laughed with him and treasured those moments of bonding and true friendship. Neither of us would dare say it, but we both knew it. Thursdays had become our favorite day of the week.

It was a Tuesday. I got word that Chaim had been taken to Beth Israel Hospital. He had experienced some chest pains and had possibly suffered a very minor heart attack. He was alert and stable, I was assured, and would return home after some routine tests. For some reason he had no phone in the hospital and could not use a cell phone there. I hesitated about visiting him, not sure if he would be entirely comfortable with an invasion of that magnitude. But then Thursday arrived.

Books in hand, I trekked to Manhattan.

> *"Chaim," I kibitzed as I entered his room, "what on earth are you doing here?"*

He popped up in his bed like a second-grade kid at the ice cream store. I wish I had brought a camera. His eyebrows seemed to jump through his head. He appeared to be stuck halfway between bewilderment and bemusement.

> *"Me?" he blurted, "what are YOU doing here?"*
> *"Chaim…it's Thursday."*

On the wall directly opposite the bed was a large clock. It read exactly 12 noon.

He looked at it. I looked at him. I thought I detected momentary and very minute eye irrigation, but it just as easily could have been my own.

Chaim looked fine — better than ever. He excused the mess in the room (as if I noticed or cared) and practically scolded me for bothering to come.

> *"They want to run one more test on me," he said, "but I think I'll skip it. I'll probably come home tomorrow."*

I pulled over one of those ridiculously oversized visitor's chairs and began reading from our usual text. Chaim instinctively reached into the top drawer of the nightstand and fumbled for something. I was surprised that he had brought a yarmulke to the hospital. It seems he had begun wearing one in order to recite a blessing whenever he ate something. I hadn't known. He offered me a leftover yogurt and some apple juice from a sealed plastic container, but this time it was my turn to refuse.

The hour sailed by. Worried that my meter had already expired, Chaim scooted me out the door. I turned around for a final glance. He was waving good-bye while motioning for me to hurry out.

The next night, Shabbos arrived peacefully. A neighbor mentioned that he had seen Chaim return home an hour earlier. I didn't stop in.

For some reason, my sleep was fitful that night. At one point, while turning in bed, I noticed some very bright lights slicing through my broken Venetian slats. I looked at my clock. It was 4:36 a.m.

I leaped from my bed to look outside. Parked in front were two fire engines, a police car and an ambulance. In seconds, my heart surged and my stomach swirled.

"CHAIM," I screamed inside!

Throwing on some clothes, I dashed down the steps and out the door. His door was wide open. I gulped. I brushed past some formless and silent faces and squeezed through the narrow corridor which led to his room. I had never seen it before.

The setting was surreal, yet strangely unremarkable — like so many typical scenes. There was Chaim on the floor, surrounded by four exhausted paramedics. They had been taking turns for over an hour — trying to resuscitate a heart already departed. I anxiously peered into the eyes of the valiant heroes, but they would not return my hopeful pleas. It was just not to be. It seems Chaim came home for Shabbos and began his eternal rest.

Minutes later, I dutifully covered him with a plain white sheet and wept.

At the funeral, I spoke about the privilege I had to befriend such a gentle, sensitive, and unassuming soul. I also asked Chaim forgiveness for having ignored him for so many years and for my inability to answer all his determined questions. I pictured him wondering what all the fuss was about.

I returned home after the burial. It was simple and dignified. The January gusts sent shivers that pierced my sadness. I tightened my scarf. The block seemed very quiet. I paused as I passed Chaim's bare hedges. I lingered in the cold for a moment. So many scenes flashed through my mind. But there could have been so many more.

You know, we never really said *"Good-bye."* I guess we each thought the other one would.

A Face in
the Window

*J*une.

Ah...June.

Tulips. Suntan lotion. Baseball. Graduations. Shavuos. Fireworks. Barbeques. Finals (finally). Summer camp. Really red watermelon. Sunglasses. Father's Day.

What a month, indeed. Someday, when they ask me to recalibrate the calendar (which, by the way, will *definitely* happen), I'm going to lop off a good 8-10 days from each of December, January, and February and add them to June. No reason in the world why the greatest month of the year shouldn't have 60 or 70 days, at least!

Until then, 30 will just have to do. Oh well.

But for me, June always had an additional significance. It contained my father's birthday. Not that he ever made much of it (and, in typical European fashion we never knew how old he was, of course), but it did add a dash of supplementary luster to an already celebratory time of year.

Come to think of it, Daddy never really made very much of Father's Day either. And since the birthday and Father's Day inevitably fell so close to each other, my brother and I usually cheated and rolled the festivities into one. Daddy just kind of smiled approvingly at our annual shortcut, perhaps gladdened that less of a fuss would be made over him. In fact, if I didn't know better, and if he hadn't been born in Poland, I'd have suspected that he orchestrated his own birth to land in the vicinity of Father's Day, precisely to escape some additional rays of limelight. He was reticent and unassuming. In short, nothing like his son.

I wonder if he was *always* unassuming. Who knows? Was he indeed born, or brought up that way, or did he become inconspicuous later in life — either in response to his war experiences or perhaps as a desperate or feeble survival tool. Maybe unobtrusive inmates had a better chance of "hiding" in the Nazi death camps. I just don't know; he never really spoke to us about his six years of hell on earth.

As Father's Day (and his birthday) approach once more, I think about this delicate and understated father of mine and I search for glimpses into his humble, yet loving soul. And I am repeatedly haunted by one most vivid and moving scene from my childhood. But first some contrast.

Several years ago, on a particularly warm Tuesday morning in very late June (yes, June), I found myself walking past a school building in my neighborhood. Lined up in the adjacent street were six idling "coach" buses, brimming with jubilant and frenzied kids. A momentary chill trickled through me. Instantly, one of my fondest childhood memories surfaced. Camp departure day had arrived.

Starting at age 9, for 13 years I had lived and breathed my camping experience, not for two months a year, but practically every single day. I was infinitely obsessed with *everything* about camp. Various scenes from camp routinely visited my dreams all year — both daytime and nocturnal ones. (Some *still* do!) So camp departure day was clearly the number one day of the year for this kid. To say that the anticipation bordered on the euphoric would probably be an understatement.

Easy to understand then, that watching those buses revving up and listening to those kids howling with glee was a gripping moment for me. But then it struck me. Something was wrong — very wrong. I felt like I was confronting one of those magazine puzzles — *"What's wrong with this picture?"*

It didn't take me long to figure it out. Something **was** wrong. There was *something missing* from the scene. The parents. Where were they?

"HEY!" I shouted internally. "YOUR CHILDREN ARE LEAVING FOR CAMP! CAN'T YOU WAIT FOR THE BUSES TO PULL OUT?"

An inappropriate sweat strangely saturated my collar. I had to find out. I watched myself running to a burly chap with a whistle. He would know.

> "Excuse me," I blurted, "I see you're going off to camp."
>
> "Leaving any minute," he offered, crushing a torn duffle bag into the final empty corner of the luggage bin.
>
> "Can I ask you a question?"
>
> "Sure."
>
> **"WHERE ARE THE PARENTS**?" I demanded!
>
> "Oh, a lot of them were here before, but they left. Work, I guess. Who knows? No big deal — these kids are in good hands."

My heart sank. "A lot of them were here?" did he say? "No big deal?" Of course it's a big deal. IT'S THE BIGGEST DEAL OF THE WHOLE DARN YEAR!

I was clearly losing it.

It took me a minute or two to fully grasp the reality of the episode before me. I guess the parents *did* have places to go. Work, appointments or otherwise. A lot of the kids do have older siblings with them. Why *should* the parents have to wait for the buses to pull out? Suitable good-byes, including kisses, nosh, and money, are presumably permitted even *prior* to the buses leaving. And maybe the kids actually *prefer* to get those mushy good-byes over with early etc., etc. What got into me?

Which brings me to that one vivid and moving experience from my past that I promised you. It happened on camp departure day. And it happened every single year, for many years.

My folks woke me early and the three of us made the 80-minute subway trek to the camp bus. As you could easily figure out, little Jackie (me) didn't get much sleep the night before, dreaming of extra-inning baseball games and stirring Friday night *zemiros* (melodies) to come. But rest was the last thing on my mind. "THE DAY" had arrived!

Freshly laundered socks, a chocolate-sprinkle sandwich, and my trusted black baseball mitt filled the "Korvette's" shopping bag I usually carried, and no matter how old I was, Mommy and Daddy had a tough time keeping pace with my determined stride to the "Stairway to Heaven," otherwise known as the camp bus.

Creased loose-leaf papers posed as official bunk signs, directing us to the appropriate lines where we received pre-boarding instructions, obligatory bunkmate introductions, and the usual warnings about throwing stuff out of the bus windows and maintaining proper decorum. But when those big bus doors flew open, we all charged full steam ahead like a herd of police dogs on a manhunt. It's a miracle that other than a lot of crushed Devil Dogs and an exploding Pepsi or two, there were no serious casualties in the mad surge of exuberant youth. I would then make my annual pilgrimage to the "back of the bus" and settle in comfortably at a vacant window seat. Seatmates changed from year to year, but it really didn't matter who was sitting with me. My focus was elsewhere.

Long forgotten, by that time, were my forlorn father and mother who, missing me already, remained obediently on the now nearly evacuated sidewalk, chatting with other similarly abandoned parents. I peered out the window and watched them. Sending me to camp was not easy for them. Not financially and not emotionally. Such is the reality for survivors of the Holocaust. Separations cut deep. I was pretty young, and I didn't understand it very well, but I knew it was a real sacrifice.

Before very long, the counselors performed the ritual roll call and head count and I knew any minute we'd be on our way. I looked once more through the open window and felt that wistful pang of exhilaration and yearning. It was a strange combination of feelings and my stomach knew it.

Mommy always wore a look that said, "Everything will be fine," but Daddy looked lost. His lips seemed to quiver and his soft eyes were no longer dry.

The engines revved up. By now all the windows were crammed with waving arms and blown kisses.

"Bye-bye!"
"See you on Visiting Day!"
"Don't forget to write!"

The wheels began their tiresome thrust. The bus lurched forward. A couple of drops of already opened soda probably spilled somewhere. And then I heard it. It was a tap on the windowpane. Strong. Determined. No…maybe frightened is a better word. It was Daddy. One final good-bye. I saw his hands fumbling in his pockets. When they emerged, they were filled with candy, gum, salted peanuts, and some loose change. He shoved them through the window, half of them spilling to the gutter below. One final chance to feed me, nurture me, hold on to me…love me.

I whipped my neck around to steal a glance at those around me. I guess I was embarrassed, but it didn't matter much. By now Daddy was **running** to keep up with the departing bus. It was the only time all year he ever ran.

Our eyes met one last time. We were both crying now. His arms flailed in surrender mode as we picked up speed. He knew the separation was inevitable and imminent. It was a race he would surely lose. I stuck my head out for one last look…and stared at the peanuts on my lap. Somehow the bus seemed very quiet.

And so went the annual scene. As I grew older, the candy matured somewhat and the change became dollars, but the loving, tearful face in the window remained the same. It was the happiest sadness I could ever feel.

The irony of the situation was that we both knew that Visiting Day would arrive in less than two weeks! It's not like I was going on some yearlong voyage to "Never-Never Land." But separations do cut deep.

What really triggered this most reserved man to unabashedly display his most shielded emotions? I don't really know. We never spoke about it. Could it have been a morbid association to the trains he had boarded en route to five different concentration camps? Or a menacing reminder of separations — final ones — that he had experienced with loved ones? Or was it some overwhelmingly painful image of the bizarre disparity between the camps he went to, and the "camp" I loved so much?

I will never know. But I think I now understand why I demanded to know where those parents were, when the buses left without them that hot Tuesday morning. And I think I know why I love June so much.

Happy Father's Day, Daddy…and Happy Birthday too…I miss you.

Zaidy Says Hello

*M*y Dear Precious One,

First of all, *Happy Birthday*!

While you are sure to hear those two words every year around this time, this is really the only time the greeting will be *precisely* true — today being the day you were actually born.

Second, welcome to the world.

How was the trip? Long? Scary? Confusing? I'm sure it was, though I don't remember mine too well. Don't worry, neither will you. That's just the way things are down here — lots of trips, loads of confusion and plenty of forgetting.

Permit me to introduce myself. I am your grandfather — your father's father. Some call me Zaidy — it's Yiddish, but it makes folks comfortable so we allow it. I'm the one who pretends to know everything, while others pretend to agree with me. That's probably because I pay the bills. Pretty soon you'll understand what I'm talking about.

Twenty-eight-and-a-half years ago I wished your father a *Happy Birthday* when he completed his trip, and today I have the privilege to do the same. I don't mind telling you it is quite a thrill. Having just returned from the hospital and seeing your 8 pounds and 11 ounces for the first time, I am filled with a special kind of joy that is most difficult to put into words.

I stood outside the nursery a few hours ago with my nose pressed against the glass, like two stuck page-corners of a new unopened book, for quite some time. I must have looked funny to you. Come to think of it, you looked pretty funny too. I just wanted to get as close as I could, I guess. Or maybe I just felt very much at home there since I was born in the very same hospital as you...er...quite a while ago. Who knows?

One thing is certain — you were clearly the most beautiful baby there. Never mind that the other "nose pressers" thought *their* babies were more special. What do *they* know? They were just jealous. And how mature you seemed, waiting patiently to be attended to and hardly complaining — unlike the girl next to you who was literally crying like a baby! I was so proud.

By the way, for your information, you are a boy. This is not insignificant, not only because I am one too, but because this evens out the score of the grandkids. You don't know them yet, but you've got some really cute first cousins and an adorable sister — which is important to keep in mind when you get home and she starts biting you.

While they didn't receive a welcome letter like this (Zaidy wasn't such a famous writer then), one day soon they will read this letter also and they will need to know that Zaidy loves them every bit as much as he does you. Somehow, grandparents never seem to run out of love.

You will find out soon enough that having a Zaidy is a pretty cool thing. And, thank G-d, you are fortunate to have four grandparents — all of whom have been charged with the mission to spoil you rotten...and they will. Believe me, I know them...they will.

A word of caution, my little bundle, you might come to take this grandparent thing for granted. Don't. When I was growing up (take note — you will hear that expression very very often), I knew only one grandparent. *Bompapa* (French/Belgian slang for *good father*) was as passionate in his Judaism as he was in his love for his family. Born in Slomnick, Poland, he moved to Antwerp during the Russo-Japanese War and there raised an exceptional family.

In 1942 they arrived in New York via France and Portugal and began the task of creating a new generation of distinction, led by *Bompapa's* fierce value system, fanciful wit, and obsession with truth and servitude. While in his early 90's, he became my roommate.

I missed out by having only one grandparent, but, believe it or not, most of my friends grew up without any grandparents at all.

Our European parents had, by and large, lost most of their nuclear families in the War and came to these benevolent shores penniless, broken, and alone. So having a grandfather (especially one in his 90's) was very special. So was he. He didn't speak much, but he didn't have to. All I had to do was watch.

Even at that advanced age, he treasured every living moment and approached everything he did with incredible commitment and vigor. The way he prayed, the way he sipped his tea, studied the Prophets, played chess, guided his daughter (my Mom — your great-grandmother)…even the way he watched wrestling, gave me a sampling that always said, *"Life is precious. Never be lazy or indifferent."* He taught me that having opinions is a good thing, and to never be ashamed or reluctant to share them.

I still recall the day he told me he was going to die. He sat up in his bed, much the way I picture the narrative of Yaakov Avinu (our Patriarch Jacob) prior to his death, and he summoned me to sit beside him. He told me to fetch his *Kiddush* cup from the dining-room breakfront. Like him, it was small, but very proud and shiny — and strong. Then, without sentiment or display of emotion, he held my hand firmly and stared deeply into my eyes. He explained that he would soon pass away, and he wanted me to own and use his *Kiddush* cup when he would use it no longer. I was 23 at the time. When he reached 100 years old, two years later, I assumed ownership of this sacred silver heirloom. And I have lovingly held it every Friday night since then.

You see, my little newcomer, that's what Judaism is really all about — linkage. Just a few hours ago, your very new soul joined a very old chain…a chain that has been growing and glowing for 5000 plus years. The chain is long and though it is tarnished in certain places, it remains as sturdy and convincing as it is durable and determined.

You will discover, my beloved, that so unusual is this chain that despite the fact that every single link is made up of different material and hue, somehow it is indestructible. Oh, many have tried to interrupt and even disintegrate this miraculous bond of conviction, beauty, and tradition, but no one ever has or ever will succeed — for so has G-d pledged.

I recently spoke with a Chassidic Jew in his late 80's, who was a childhood friend of my father, of blessed memory. After recounting several anecdotes of life growing up in Poland, his soft, pale-blue eyes became wistful as he recalled his years of tragedy in Auschwitz. He stroked his gleaming, white beard and peered out the window. He seemed to be gazing into a time long passed.

"I lost everyone there...everyone. When the War ended, I was completely alone."

He paused and said nothing for a few seconds. The silence made me uncomfortable. Then he leaned forward on his bent swivel chair and whispered softly.

"I cannot tell you the number, but today I have between 300 and 400 children, grandchildren and great-grandchildren. It is a miracle."

And now you are a part of that very same miracle — the miracle of survival — the miracle we call "the Jewish People." Today, you take your place in this vaulted legacy and start your journey as yet another link in our priestly union. But unlike me and my little colleagues of yesteryear, you begin, not only with loving and devoted parents, but also with the benefit of many adoring grandparents and even great-grandparents at your side.

I suggest you take full advantage of this benefit. Watch us. Learn from (much of) what we do and don't do. Ask us questions and don't accept vague or confusing answers. Request our help with your homework and with school projects. Pester us to play games with you. (We are notorious for letting you win.) Invite yourself over just to hang around for an hour or two and occasionally to sleep over...and bring your baseball glove with you. Call us on a cold, winter night just to say, "Hi, what's doing?" Fax us a copy of a great composition you wrote or a "98" (or even a "75") on a recent *Chumash* (Bible) test. And every now and then, ask us about our lives when we were younger. We just love to reminisce.

It isn't fun to think about, but someday I'll pass that *Kiddush* cup on to you — or one of your cousins. Don't cry — that's just the way life is on this world. In a way, it's even a comforting thought. As I said before, it's all about the chain. And today that chain got just a little bit stronger.

Welcome.

The Three Most Important Words in the World

I don't have much patience for speeches.

Look around at the audience (as I often do), and you'll notice how fidgety and uncomfortable most people are... provided they are awake. Hair twirling, lint picking, and yawn hiding are the usual fare, among others.

But by far, the most convenient and suddenly fascinating phenomenon ever discovered is the human fingernail. This relatively simple anatomic marvel can provide hours of infinitely versatile opportunities for distraction. And we've got TEN OF THEM!

So there I was, in row 41, seat 7. I was just finishing a particularly creative oral manicure of my left pinky cuticle, when my ears perked up. The speaker, a close friend of mine (that's why I *had* to be there), posed a question that stopped my fingernail designing right in its tracks.

> *"What are the three most important words in a marriage?"*
> *"Easy," I thought. " I love you."*
> *"And they are not, 'I love you,'" he added.*

The audience stirred. Hair twirling was suspended. Even some lint pickers took notice. I could hear everybody's mind working.

"What could be more important than 'I love you'? What phrase could he possibly be talking about? Could any three words really save a marriage?"

My mind raced with the others'. Surely I can come up with a few possibilities of my own.

> *"You getting that?"*
> *"YOU'RE really tired???"*
> *"I was shaving."*

Thankfully, he put us out of our collective anticipatory misery relatively quickly.

"The three most important words in a marriage are, **'I was wrong.'"**

A lot of heads nodded. Count mine among them. A chord had been struck. According to Dr. Meir Wikler, no single phrase can elevate and cultivate a relationship more than the ability to admit one's wrongdoing. Spouse...colleague...sibling...boss...committee...friend...perhaps even parent. No matter what the context of the association, admitting you were wrong can add an immeasurable dimension to the connection. It's refreshing, honest, disarming, and frequently unexpected.

And yet, admitting one's fault, in deed, thought or perception, is probably among the most difficult chores we have to face. Why? Why are most of us so bent on ALWAYS being right? Are our egos so frail and fragile that they cannot endure even the *occasional* admission of fault?

Apparently...yes. Our egos *are* indeed frail, fragile, flimsy and feeble.

So fearful are we of any exposure of weakness, that our defense mechanisms kick into high gear faster than you could say, "Oops...I blew it!"

Our entire defensive structure is actually so sophisticated that when confronted with the dismal prospect of having to face our own lapses and oversights, we often shift into denial, in order to evade the dreaded revelation that we are flawed in any way.

Excuse mechanisms, at times exotically creative, and often bordering on outright lying, are quickly conjured up.

> *"I didn't mean it that way."*
> *"I did not forget. You once told me you preferred if I don't*

buy you an anniversary present."

"*I can't believe it! I was just about to call you back!*"

You get the idea. It is as if our entire sense of self — our emotional equilibrium — is virtually dependent on never being wrong about anything. What's more, often times we end up convincing ourselves that our excuse, our defensiveness, or the lie was actually true, or, at the very least, justified. That's how intolerable it is, for so many of us, to accept and admit our imperfections or failings.

We need look no further than our own White House for a prime example of the total incapability of individuals to utter those precious three words, despite the overwhelming evidence of transgression and potential for resolution that acknowledgment of guilt would have generated. Instead, the hole just gets deeper and deeper.

Our universal resistance to admitting fault becomes even more enigmatic when you consider that we have all experienced that rare occasion when some surprisingly secure soul comes along and actually says, "I was wrong." Like the athlete, mercilessly stalked in the losing team's locker room for the post-game interview, who stoically mutters into dozens of microphones and millions of living rooms, "*I blew it. I take full responsibility for our defeat out there today.*"

What is our unmitigated response to that person?

"*He's a hero!*" we proclaim.

"*What inner strength...fortitude...courage does he possess!*"

Our admiration for that individual is boundless, but somehow it falls short from encouraging us to do likewise. Like the doctor's needle, we shun the obvious benefits awaiting us and see only the momentary pain it causes.

But Judaism makes every attempt to set us on the right path. We are infused with the concept that acknowledging our culpability is not only praiseworthy, it is also curative. We become accustomed to recognizing our own mistakes by mentioning them in our prayers every day. And the *holiest* day of the year, Yom Kippur, is distinguished by our ability to *honestly* admit our shortcomings. It is the *extent* of that sincerity that greatly determines the forgiveness we receive.

So here's my suggestion.

Let's try it. Once a day. Perhaps for two weeks or so. Take a deep breath...close your eyes and whisper, "I was wrong."

And then open your eyes and bask in the smiles of bewilderment around you. (Or at least try it in the mirror when no one's around.)

And watch your wings grow.

Out of the Woods

*L*ike a clap of thunder on a scorching August night, it shook me. Could it really be true? Could it actually happen?

It sounded more like a plot from a novel for young adolescents. A teenage girl, torn from her surroundings, is suddenly thrust into the spotlight of frantic search teams, as fears for her survival abound. And yet, reality was more frightening than fiction.

News of Sharon reverberated through scores of Jewish communities everywhere. And the reactions all reflected similar sentiment, albeit in varying tones.

> *"How could such a thing happen?"*
> *"It's an emergency for every single Jew!"*
> *"Let's get mobilized!"*
> *"Every second counts!"*

The response was incredible…unprecedented! Jews from every neighborhood, every persuasion, every generation vaulted into spontaneous action. Search teams were organized, schedules were synchronized, buses were rented, thousands gathered to hear words of *chizuk* and to say *Tehillim.* People who had never volunteered for anything in their lives found themselves in positions of leadership. Thousands of cheeks were stained with inexplicable tears. A wave of compulsion to *DO SOMETHING* pervaded our lives.

And all this for a girl whom most of us never knew, never met, never will meet. Sharon, whose soul, like millions of other wandering souls, was only waiting for someone to care enough. A living testimony to *"Mi ke'amcha Yisrael, goy echad baaretz — Who is like Your people, Israel, one nation in the land!"*

Even the most ardent critics could not help but rave.
"Such concern!"
"Such commitment!"
"They don't even know the kid!"

The world gaped at the sight of thousands of "strangers" trading slumber for sacrifice, work for worry, and learning for love. Amidst the decadence of a universe in which the value of human life faces a constant downward spiral, a display of such compassion should make headlines. And it did. *"Annu ratzim, v'heim ratzim* — We run and they run."

But the most spectacular aspect of this incredible rescue effort was the fact that Sharon's life was never in danger. After all, this is 1995. This was no Suri Feldman situation. That was last year's crisis. Oh, the danger for Sharon's survival was very real. And the situation was quite critical. But, unlike Suri, Sharon's physical existence was never threatened. This time, the very notion that a Jewish girl was "lost," had "strayed from the path" of her heritage and faced spiritual extinction, was enough to spin the wheels of *Hatzalah* along with everyone else, in motion once again.

Of course, Suri's disappearance last year will never be forgotten. And in truth, we owe her a great debt. For our efforts in finding her taught us the lesson that we had long ago forgotten, and made this current mission possible. Who would have thought that the same enthusiasm that had catapulted a People to the heights of devotion just one year ago, could once again be harnessed for the sake of spiritual rescue?

The lesson is clear. When a Jewish soul is lost, all of *Klal Yisrael* must hurt. And when a *neshamah* strays into the forest of assimilation, no one should be able to sleep. Maybe that was her *kavannah* when she was praying in the woods. She wanted us to look for all the "lost" children.

Thanks, Suri. I guess we needed that.

Under G-d's Canopy

*D*ear Shmuel,

It all happens tonight. In about 10 hours from now you will be a married man.

Wait. Let me write that again.

In about 10 hours from now you will be a married man.

Thank you. I just needed to let that sink in, though I have a feeling it might take considerably more time for that to happen.

Tonight it will be just you and Reena...finally...standing under your very own *chuppah*, looking out on 600 or so of your closest friends and relatives, who will leap to their feet in joy and unison (*"Mazel Tov!"*) when they hear that glass break.

Off to the side will stand Mommy and I. We'll be doing the whimpering thing. Even though you are our fourth child to be married, we have earned our crying stripes and we may well take full advantage. You won't really notice us. Your focus will be elsewhere, as it should be. That's O.K. — it's about time I let someone else take the spotlight.

Just a few minutes earlier we will have walked you down the aisle, each of us clutching one of your arms, as if trying to hold on to our *little boy* for the last time. But when the march concludes and the band goes quiet, we *will* let go...I promise. And you will climb the steps of true independence, for that is truly the fulfillment of our dream for you.

In those few moments under G-d's canopy, everything will change. You will welcome Reena to stand beside you. What a marvelous choice you have made — she is beautiful both inside and out.

Finding one single, definitive way to send you off with the perfect life perspective is nearly impossible. Hopefully, having lived with us for 23 years, you already know something about what we consider to be life's priorities, goals, and problem-solving methodologies.

Rather, my thoughts today are simply about love — the love of a father to his son — from me to you. So many loving images dart before my eyes as I try to capture (and preserve) those special moments. And a lot of what I cherish about you are qualities of your personality that others have similarly noticed and appreciated. Who hasn't enjoyed your easy laugh, your gentle disposition, and your kind and tender temperament?

Arguing with you was usually a one-way street, as your disarming manner and oh-so-logical mind just wouldn't cooperate with everyone else's sparring inclinations. And when the persistent will of others would just refuse to capitulate, you always seemed to find it so easy to be the one to *just give in*. What a beautiful feature! How can we not love you for that?

Growing up in a big family like you did, and being in the middle of the pack, is not easy. You have to be a big brother to some, the little brother to others, and usually end up with the privileges of neither. Somehow, you wore the uniform perfectly. It just didn't bother you. Never too demanding, rarely complaining, and always ready to extend yourself to anyone else's whim. I'm not quite sure how you managed it all, but you did — and everyone adored you for achieving that unusual balance.

Shmuel, we survivors on the home front are going to miss that. We'll miss that at the Shabbos table, at dinner, and at our "midnight and beyond" laughing sessions. But you have a chance to further utilize those special qualities to make your own home a haven for that unique brand of kindness and serenity. Not coincidentally, I have already detected many of those very same traits in Reena. So you have a rare opportunity to meld those attributes you both hold precious, to forge a happy, calm, and secure living environment. I have a feeling it will work.

The only additional essential ingredient to your mix is, of course, G-d.

"Blessed are You, L-rd, our G-d, King of the universe, Who has created everything for His glory."

This is the very first blessing recited to you after your marriage. Curious. While no one would doubt the veracity of the claim — the world is G-d's and His honor is supreme — why do we choose to inaugurate your life together with this obvious reminder?

Our Sages knew what they were doing. Tonight you are truly the *Big Man on Campus*. That's fine. Every note, every wish, every flashbulb, every toast, every embrace, and even every envelope truly belongs to you and Reena. And that's the way it should be. This is your moment together.

In fact, that's the way it's been since your engagement, some three months ago. Despite our busy home, lately everything else has kind of played second fiddle to *"THE WEDDING!"* All this is rather wonderful, but it is also potentially dangerous. With so much focus, so much attention, and heck, *so much money* thrown your way, you might (subconsciously, of course) begin to actually believe that the world revolves around you. It's hard *not* to think that way.

Of course, it is this much-distorted perception that has ruined many a good marriage. Precisely at the time when you need most to shift your egocentric patterns and begin a life of true sharing and selflessness, you are put to the real test.

And so, in full cognizance of this pressing need, our Sages wanted to remind you — right from the start — that those days are over. Marriage is not an exercise in self-indulgence. It is a holy union, one that must not only include, but *highlight* G-d in every fiber of your newfound coexistence. He is not a silent partner or an innocent bystander of your relationship. He is, in fact, the *very essence* of why you have been destined to share your lives together.

This opening blessing is a proclamation of this essential life tenet. It is one that we hope you have witnessed yourself, growing up in our home. May you both be blessed with the strength, the insight, and the tranquility to live and breathe with that constant reality.

Shmuel, my dear son, tonight you and I will experience every emotion that a father and son can possibly experience: joy, fear, pride, longing, separation, unification, ambivalence, reminiscence and delight...to name a few. We will dance with many partners, all of whom represent a relationship that has meant something important to each of us.

But there is sure to be a moment — and it may not last very long — when you and I will dance together and our eyes will meet. Mine are sure to be restless and moist; yours will be determined and reassuring. I hope to cherish that moment forever.

And when the guests have all parted and the drummer has wrapped up his cymbals of joy; and when the petals have long been trampled on and the final kisses have been firmly planted; and when the checkroom has only empty hangers and the serenade strains are no longer wafting in the melancholy air, you and I will bid farewell.

Mommy and I will watch as you and Reena disappear into married life. Please...do me one small favor. Don't look back. We'll be O.K. Our throats may lump a bit and our stomachs may churn, but that will pass. Tonight is about you and Reena...nothing else.

See you later, kid.

Don't forget the ring.

Love always,

Tatty

Friends Don't Grow on Trees

*F*riends.

Our search, our desire, and our need to surround ourselves with people we can share our lives with, begins when we are not yet verbal and seems to never ever end.

At times, it seems that our very existence is frequently dominated by the friends we have or have not. We long for friends; we require friends. We yearn for friends; we pine for friends. Friends can give us reason to live...to cry...to emulate...to strive...to show off...to play...to be silly...and to be somber.

What power!

And yet, defining exactly from where this immense might really emanates is elusive. Think of your three closest friends and try to identify the role they play in your life. Not so easy, is it? Now try to imagine experiencing any event of your life, of even minor significance, without any good friend with you. What could be more sad?

But attaining success in this most critical pursuit is far from automatic. We are all familiar with people who are surrounded with loads of good, loyal friends, while others know of no such circle. Instead, they shuffle along, pretending to love their autonomy and solitude *("you can't really count on anyone but yourself")*, while they suffer in silence — alone, dispirited, and secretly afraid of tomorrow.

The question is, *"Why?"* Why are some people seemingly *blessed* with wonderful, wise, and caring friends while so many others somehow appear *destined* for loneliness?

The question is a troubling one. Not only because it affects so many people so profoundly, but because it calls into focus the ageless quandary about G-d's role in predetermining our lives vs. our own efforts in causing our successes and failures. What is the reality? Are some people really *blessed* with those great relationships? Are others actually *destined* for a life of insipid isolation?

Great minds have grappled with this most central life question throughout the millennia. Philosophical literature and responsa are replete with attempts at unlocking the mystery of exactly how much G-d intervenes and determines our destiny and our decisions in life. While far from being an authority on this most confounding topic, I can state one truism about it. Not too many of us ever did or ever will fully understand it.

What does seem clear, however, is that few, if any, events in our personal lives occur without both of these dynamics at play. In other words, just about everything that happens to us, happens as a result of a combination of G-d's will and our own efforts.

For example, no one ever became a millionaire by collecting tolls on the Bayonne Bridge. Becoming exceedingly wealthy usually requires a plan of action, a failure or three, and a heckuva lot of effort. And then some Divine intervention, as well (or a very rich and deceased uncle). And yet, many follow the *exact* same formula and still come up empty-handed.

Similarly, it's unfair to expect to live a long, healthy life while you constantly feast on pastrami burgers, Cajun fries, deep chocolate mousse, and pancake syrup, never leave your couch except to meander over to the microwave, smoke three packs a day, and face constant financial and emotional stress. Of course, here too, we all know people, some of them in their 80's or above, who seem to be doing just that. (We probably can't stand them!)

In other words, there are no guarantees. Usually we just play the percentages. In finances, health and countless other crucial areas in life we realize G-d has the final say, but we need to do our fair share. And then we pray and hope for the best. Very reasonable.

But not everything should be approached that way. There are certain facets of our existence that seem to be weighted more to one side or the other.

For instance, while cosmetics, clothes, style, and grooming can certainly help, a person's overall attractiveness is probably more dictated by G-d than by his own efforts. Frustrating, perhaps, but true nonetheless. And you might think you have "lucky" numbers or are privy to some incredible "system," but whether or not you win the lottery is clearly more in the Divine domain than in yours. Sorry. And perhaps even more obviously, whether someone is prone to allergies or not has very little to do with how many vitamins he takes. These things and others have more to do with G-d's choices for us than our efforts for ourselves.

Conversely, it could be argued that while people may be born with predispositions toward certain character traits (kindness, sensitivity, patience, etc.), more often than not, *we* are responsible for our behavior. The more work *we* put into perfecting our temperament and disposition, the more perfect they are likely to become. Sure, G-d's help is always important, but it seems that when it comes to our moral fiber we hold the needle and thread.

So, sometimes G-d is mainly running the show, sometimes we are, and sometimes it seems more equally balanced.

And now we come to friendship. Into which category does that seem to best fit? Many or most people appear to have referred this department to the Supervisor Himself. As we said earlier, some of us are *blessed* with many wonderful friends; others are *destined* to relative solitude.

Frankly, I disagree.

Akiva, a friend of mine, heard that a rabbi of note was moving into his neighborhood some years ago. He had enjoyed a casual and infrequent relationship with him, but always dreamed of developing it into a true friendship. He didn't wait for the rabbi to move in and then "see what happens." He didn't count on serendipity (G-d) to orchestrate their paths crossing. He actually sat down and wrote him a letter *before* he moved — welcoming him to the neighborhood and suggesting they plan a once-a-week one-hour study session, after the move.

Fact is, the rabbi turned down Akiva's initial request, for some reason. But the letter was heartily appreciated and it launched their current friendship of note.

Friendship is neither a luxury, nor a burden, nor a symptom of unresolved childhood dependency issues. It is an essential component of the human condition. Yes — some need friends more, some less. But even the Sages of the Mishnah — some 1800 plus years ago — implored us to *"Accept a teacher upon yourself and acquire a friend"* (*Ethics of the Fathers* 1:6).

And acquiring friends does not mean waiting at home for your cell phone to vibrate, and then deploring your *bad fortune* when you feel alone. Acquisitions of this kind require serious motivation, very specific strategies, and the courage to risk. It isn't easy to lay bare your vulnerabilities and chance rejection. Often you need to summon up some hefty doses of *chutzpah* to approach someone you barely know and strike up a conversation, ask a question, or invite him/her to an event. And circumstances — real ones, like age, time, neighborhood, cliques, financial standing, shyness, bad breath, etc. — frequently present formidable obstacles to overcome. But it's worth the effort.

The point to remember is that life is just too complicated and fragile to go it alone. Everyone needs at least a mini Advisory Board these days. And hoping, praying, or expecting these friendships to breed and develop on their own is unrealistic at best, precarious at worst.

Taking an active role in this crucial hunt means sitting down with pen, paper and brain, and thinking about who, within your personal radar, would be a really valuable addition to your address book. Crude and unromantic as it may sound, specific tactics then need to be formulated and implemented in order to increase your chances of establishing a meaningful friendship.

"But doesn't G-d just sort of put people together if they belong together?," I hear you asking. Yes…sometimes. But more often than not, *you* need to do most of the work. And, all the more so, the same work ethic applies afterwards — when you want to make the friendship meaningful, satisfying, and lasting.

G-d can help. But *you* must make it happen.

That's just the way it is.

Connecting
the Unattached

I. THE SCOPE OF THE PROBLEM

*A*new era has clearly dawned. While claims of total isolation from the narcissistic tugs of American culture would certainly be an overstatement, Torah Judaism has not surrendered! *Chessed* projects in nearly every category imaginable have abounded, reaching unanticipated heights. Bikur Cholim, Dial-A-Chavrusa, *hachnasas kallah,* Hatzolah, *kiruv rechokim,* The Yitti Leibel Helpline, *gemachs,* etc. have all emerged as a formidable collective response to the "Me Generation."

And yet, our purview might still be too narrow. We might do well to adjust our blinds (both proverbial and vertical) somewhat and discover who it is that is living right next door. Chances are (and the odds are growing) that person might be in his/her late 20's, 30's or even 40's, and single. The unattached Orthodox population, including divorcees and widows, besides those who've never experienced the *kedushah* of a *chuppah,* is swiftly becoming greater in numbers and in pain than anyone could have ever predicted. But somehow, very few of us really notice them.

Statistics reflecting the actual number of Orthodox singles are unreliable and ambiguous at best...depressing and tragic at worst.

Indisputable, however, is the fact that many thousands of high-functioning, sensitive men and women in our midst suffer immeasurably from their spouse-less status. Many choose to suffer in silence. Others simply have no choice. As one single woman put it, "Please be extra careful with my feelings...I have no one waiting at home to cry to."

And their anguish is rarely self-contained. More often than not, there are heartbroken and confused parents whose agony frequently surpasses that of their older, single children. Even siblings and extended family are not immune to the "long arm" of complexities caused by the tribulations of being single in a community and a heritage that is so family oriented.

The purpose of this article, then, is to highlight some of the problems that are peculiar to *frum* singles, inject some theory as to why we fail to notice them sufficiently, and offer some suggestions for amelioration of their pain.

∞ LONELINESS

The *Ribbono Shel Olam* did not create this world for man to live alone. Companionship and affection of marriage are incontrovertible ingredients for happiness in this world. And while loneliness and isolation are, unfortunately, all too commonplace even within certain marriages, only the single himself can ever experience the full impact of life alone.

Among the singles I have known, both professionally and otherwise, the experience of loneliness is practically universal.

One woman, divorced for four years, found herself at home one Yom Tov...alone:

"There I was in my dining room making *Kiddush* for myself on the second night of Yom Tov unsure of the halachah of saying *Shehecheyanu*...or whether I really even wanted to."

Another women described the loneliness this way:

"What really hurts is the loneliness of carrying all the responsibilities alone, not having anyone to share concerns with — minor concerns, minor worries, incidental problems — and the minor triumphs. Also, lacking someone to whom I am the most important person — not to be making a major difference in someone else's life. To feel that if I weren't there, no one would really notice the difference. I often wonder if I'll ever get married and why Hashem would let me be alone; and then I wonder how soon Mashiach will come."

Do we truly fathom the depths of their loneliness? Commiserating with a single with a remark like: "I know how lonely you must feel," is usually regarded as downright insulting.

⌒ ESTRANGEMENT

In a world so totally geared toward marriage and children, singles feel disjointed and strange — or perhaps more accurately, estranged, since that is what our treatment of them suggests. Somehow they just don't fit in.

A 34-year-old explained it this way:

> "I feel so out of place in shul with everyone wearing a tallis except me. But the worst is Simchas Torah when everybody brings their kids — and I watch them dancing, sitting on their Tatty's shoulders and laughing. And I say, 'Wow — I should be doing that!' But I just don't know if I will."

One 36-year-old single woman told me:

> "No matter what you do, you're not really part of the community. Marriage is the greatest sense of belonging that you could have: after that, there's a community. But you're not really viewed as a full-fledged member of Klal Yisrael! Frankly, I can't remember having sinned so badly that I should be 36 and still single."

Further alienation is often caused, inadvertently, by the marriage of a close friend, when a host of mixed feelings emerge within the friend who remains single. As one woman put it:

> "Honestly speaking, it's a big loss when a friend gets married, I find I have to walk a very fine line between mourning that loss and trying to be happy for the other person — not letting my disappointment get in the way of their joy."

⌒ CONDEMNATION

Most glaring, however, is the feeling the singles get of blame and condemnation for their predicament. Frequently, seemingly innocent exchanges with others reflect an undercurrent of the position of many, that their singlehood is their own fault and they must bear the responsibility for it and be punished.

☜ STEREOTYPE

Many of us are guilty of lumping all singles together into one giant stereotypical profile — as we tend to do with certain professionals, races or Bais Yaakovs. Time after time I hear the familiar refrain of the singles saying:

"We're people, we're individuals. Find out who I am; judge me by my merits. Labels can't be used to define individuals — it doesn't tell you who the person is." One woman described the community's evaluation as simply, "You're a child until you're married."

II. NEGLECT: WHY?

If, as was previously noted, we are so mindful and prudent with our *chessed* responsibilities toward other less-fortunate souls, why is it that the singles somehow come up short? Clearly, our "overextended" schedules do not curtail our vigilant involvement in other areas!

Ignorance, you say? I think not, since one would have to be totally blind not to notice them wherever we go.

Oh no, singles. It's not as if we don't know you exist. We see you ...We see you in shul — on both sides of the mechitzah — without a tallis, without a sheitel or a ring, We see you in the bakery buying one small egg challah on Erev Shabbos. We see you on visiting day in camp, walking alone, or in a bungalow colony, driving into the parking lot with your sub-compact Mazda without infant seats in the back. Oh, we see you...Or do we?

Well, we *must* see you. We often comment: "There's Srully — is he still around?" "There's that divorced woman — what's her name? *Ach* — so young, *nebbich.*" So we *do* see you. It's just that we'd rather not! You make us feel guilty for not doing more. You make us feel unworthy for having what you don't have. You make us feel inadequate because we don't really know what to say to you; or, perhaps more important, what *not* to say to you. So we play it safe. We ignore you.

Or we tend to play down the situation. Almost everyone who discusses *shidduchim* has an interesting way of referring to the proposed individuals. It's usually: "I have a nice boy for you to meet." or: "She's a really good girl."

These people might be 35 or 40 years old, but they are still referred to as "boys" or "girls" — or as a *"feiner bochur"* or a *"shayna maidel."* It's as if we all want to believe that they're really adolescents. Of course, a 20-year-old boy, once he's married, is suddenly a *"yunger man"*!

It's a collective denial designed for the comfort of all. We call them boys and girls to keep them young, negate the truth, and thus dilute the imperative. But the stark reality is that the ascendancy of the single population is a terrible discomfort and a tragedy for everyone.

One patient of mine, a single man in his late 30's, revealed during a session that for the previous three to four months, he had begun leaving shul during *krias haTorah.*

"I'm just sick and tired," he said, "of hearing the *gabbai's* voice calling me for an *aliyah,* referring to me as 'habochur' or 'hachassan.' The *kibitzing* that follows hurts too much."

This vignette is not meant as a vote for changing the sacred *"Hilchos Gabboyis,"* but rather as a glimpse into the beaten psyche of a veteran single...we can at least empathize.

And we ignore this issue for another, perhaps more sensitive reason. We feign unawareness to delude ourselves into believing that we and our families are immune to this "singles disease." But, of course, such is not the case.

Last year my wife and I were privileged to be among the hosts of a Shabbaton, sponsored by the Kesher organization.

Approximately forty high-functioning, *frum* eligibles were able to meet in a non-pressured Shabbos atmosphere. At *Shalosh Seudos* one young lady, 28 years old, spontaneously rose to thank the hosts for their efforts and hospitality. It was, she said later, her public speaking debut. "Although I didn't find my *bashert* this Shabbos," she said, "I thank you for trying. And in the merit of your efforts, may you and your children never be faced with the sadness that we experience everyday."

She sat down in the quiet room. But the thoughts of all the hosts spoke out loudly. Until now we thought we were practicing *gemillas chessed* for them. Now we realize how scared we are for *ourselves.* Suddenly it wasn't just them...it could also be us.

III. SHAPING THE IMPERATIVE

When singles are asked what the community should be doing for them, there is little unanimity in their responses.

One 35-year-old fellow told me, "The best thing you can do for singles is help them not be single anymore."

On the other hand, one 34-year-old woman said, "When we want to get married, we will. *HaKadosh Baruch Hu* takes care of that. We just need help surviving until then."

But a few basic guidelines are in order. These measures must be prefaced, however, with the statement of fact that the repair process has already begun. A number of organizations have begun to address the needs of this special group. And everyday, more and more sensitive and caring individuals are opening their homes, their hearts, and their mouths in demonstration of support for the unattached. But, it's not enough.

1. OUTREACH

One obvious necessity is the need to seek them out. Singles will rarely approach you and force their own integration. Most people know many singles, besides the countless familiar strangers that we frequently encounter but never dare approach. Extend a hand to them. A smile. An invitation. Make them feel wanted.

"It's nice when people are receptive when I invite myself over for Shabbos," one single told me, "but it doesn't compare to getting a call from them that says 'I'm thinking of you. You mean something to us.' "

And those fortunate families (and there are many) who do share a Shabbos meal, a Purim *seudah,* or a dreidel game with those who usually sit alone, agree that their own family life is enhanced immeasurably. Yes. Givers are takers.

2. MATCHMAKING

Compiling a list of the Do's and Don't's of matchmaking is better left to more qualified and experienced persons and to more space than this article permits. Unfortunately, we often hide behind our imperfections and decide to forego *"redding shidduchim"* entirely. "I'm not good at that sort of thing" may be an honest remark, but it's still an invalid excuse. Having doubts about one's capacity to be the perfect parent is hardly reason enough for not having children.

And yet, the *shadchanus* industry is often treated with such fragility — as if there is no room for error.

Kiruv rechokim, a process of increasing complexity and specialization, is nevertheless one that everyone can be a part of, notwithstanding the expected blunders that may ensue. Similarly, most people who are quite capable of recommending that two people should meet, rarely even try it. Of course, careful consideration and good common sense are prerequisites for any proposed matchmaking, but laser-optic surgery it is not. Any "damage" done is rarely irreparable.

Ironically, it is often those people who do not venture into this territory, who are also the best connected and most likely to know the most people. No license or *semichah* required.

Just remember the reply that the Chofetz Chaim gave when his *talmid* complained that he had no desire to learn. "What's the problem?" asked the Chofetz Chaim. "So learn without desire!'"

Try it!

3. TAP A NATURAL RESOURCE

Include singles in your vocational, social, and organizational projects. Far too often, qualified, sensitive and dynamic candidates who happen not to be married are totally ignored when opportunities for employment and organizational fulfillment arise.

Intelligent, often brilliant singles are not even considered, when their selection — had they been married — might have been obvious. Not to mention that their schedules are frequently less time-restrictive than those with large families. They're a vibrant but untapped resource to be used in all sorts of school, community and *chessed* projects. They just need our encouragement. The outcome is usually *zeh neheneh v'zeh neheneh* — everyone gains.

4. ACCEPTANCE

Finally, and perhaps most significantly, singles need to feel accepted. And that requires our calling upon an old fashioned skill: listening. We need to remind ourselves that they are people — not statistics.

Some *shadchanim* act as if it is their life's mission to get someone married — somehow forgetting that they never got to know that person. Yes, we would like singlehood to gain the status of an endangered species, but sometimes we forget that they are people — not bald eagles.

As one single put it: "The best people to talk to are those who don't judge you. What hurts the most is that in order to stay alive, I have to use defense mechanisms all the time."

One of the simplest and most poignant comments I heard about this was from a woman who said, "I was so happy when I got married; now I could please one person instead of the whole world."

Inquire — don't interrogate. Listen — don't judge. Validate — don't incriminate. Consult — don't insult.

So when you wrap yourself in your *tallis* tomorrow morning — think about those who don't.

And when you put on that *sheitel* — make sure it doesn't cover your eyes.

Searching for Roni

I have always been reluctant to make this story public, probably because of its ending. But I believe that the time has come. I'm not sure why.

I think it was Elie Wiesel who said that G-d loves stories. I guess that's why He made airplanes. So there I was, boarding a Tower Air (remember them?) flight home from Tel Aviv to JFK. The year was 1998 and the time was 12:30 a.m. on a Friday morning. I was lugging one carry-on too many and was trying a little too hard not to make eye contact with the flight attendant. Naturally, my scheme had the opposite effect and he said something in Hebrew that sounded like I was being arrested.

I stashed my duty-free bag into another odd-shaped container I was lugging and proceeded to my seat. Someone else was sitting in it. We compared boarding passes — duplicates. Standing in the bulk-head, awaiting my new seat assignment, I watched the frenzied passengers boarding. I generously offered to sit in first class, if no other coach space was available. They were not amused.

After being displaced from yet another potential seat, I began to contemplate that perhaps G-d was somehow attempting to say a little something here. There seemed to be a very special seat waiting for me on this plane and we were not going to take off until I was correctly placed.

He was tall and dark and about 27 years old. He was in 17A. I was in 17B. We took off.

Let me clear the record. I am not a raving missionary, evangelist, or "*nuj.*" When I fly, more often than not, I am borderline anti-social. I sleep. I read. I write. I drink my Diet Pepsi with too much ice and I do not spill. I disdain small talk and am not interested in your comments about the weather, the in-flight service, world politics, or the Supreme Court.

That night, things were different. He was reading a sports magazine and looked only mildly annoyed that the seat beside him was not going to remain unoccupied. I smiled sheepishly. The first hour of the 12-hour flight passed without words. I kept busy fiddling with my earphones and my blindfold; he drifted off — catching a few winks before the meal service began.

I no longer recall how the conversation began, but it wasn't awkward. His name was Roni, he lived in Jerusalem, and attended pharmacy school in Hebrew University. After a minute or two, I breathed deeply and bravely inquired about the nature of his trip to New York.

> "*You'll laugh when I tell you,*" he said with a moderate Israeli accent.
>
> "*Great. I love to laugh.*"
>
> "*O.K. You see, I'm a really big fan of professional basketball and I follow many of the U.S. teams in the N.B.A. (National Basketball Association). A few weeks ago Michael Jordan...eh...you do know who...*
>
> "*Yes, of course — His Airness — Michael Jordan — greatest basketball player who ever laced a pair of Nikes.*"
>
> "*Yes...so Jordan announced his retirement at the end of this season and I decided that I had to see him play once, in person, before it was too late.*" So, I have a friend in Philadelphia, and we are going on Tuesday night to see him play.*"

He was wrong. I didn't laugh. I found it rather...quaint, shall we say, or maybe curious.

Out of Mr. Jordan, there ensued a rather friendly, if not absorbing conversation between us. Roni and I talked sports and travel and family and Jewish geography and Israeli politics etc. In short, we talked about everything except...religion. I guess you could say we were "hitting it off."

There were about 2 hours left to the interminable trip and my curiosity got the best of me. I swallowed hard and rammed the words through my larynx.

"So, did you have any religious education growing up?"

I waited for the plane to rumble or his little tray table to crack. Neither happened.

"None," he said almost sadly. "Not long ago, I asked my father why he had not exposed me to any religious studies. He said because when he grew up he was forced to attend classes related to religious instruction. He thought that was wrong and would not subject me to the same coercive tactics."

"And what did you answer him?"

"I told him that by denying me the choice, he had actually done the exact same thing to me that his parents had done to him."

He was sharp, no question about it. And his answer gave me an opening to take our conversation a bit further. I did.

"So, it sounds like you feel a bit deprived — like you missed out on something."

"Naw...not really," he countered. "I don't have much interest anyway."

Well, I thought, so much for that.

I consider it a privilege, more than a duty, to share some of the fulfillment I experience from my religion, with those who never had the opportunity. But Roni's curtains seemed kind of drawn. I withdrew.

It was about half an hour later when Roni turned to me.

"Do you know how long it takes to get to the Port Authority bus station from JFK airport?"

"About 45 minutes by bus," I responded. "Are you taking a bus to Philadelphia?"

"Actually, no. I'm going to a friend of mine in Montreal for the weekend and then going to Philly for the big game on Tuesday."

There was less than an hour left to landing. For some odd reason, I decided to go for one more try.

"Roni," I stammered, *"I hope you won't think this is strange, but I'd like to ask you a question, but I don't really want an answer."*

"Selichah?" (pardon me) he replied...puzzled. "You don't want me to answer your question?"

"Well, not just yet. I want to ask you something, but I'd prefer if you waited a full 5 minutes before you answered me."

"O.K. Shoot."

(I guess he was comfortable using basketball terminology.)

"How about...instead of going to Montreal, I know it sounds strange, you come to my house in Brooklyn and spend Shabbos with my family and me. I've got nice private accommodations for you, incredible food, and adorable kids. I even have a small basketball court in the back! Remember, think for 5 minutes before you answer."

Roni did not seem fazed. He just wasn't a "fazed" type of guy. He did laugh, though. He looked about 65 percent amused and 30 percent stupefied. (I leave the other 5 percent to you.) But to his credit, he didn't answer. He even looked like he was thinking about it. We both just waited...quietly...not very comfortably. Finally, after about 30 minutes, 5 minutes had passed.

"Thanks for the invitation. It's really very nice of you, but, as I said, my friend in Montreal is expecting me. Maybe some other time."

I was not disappointed. I didn't really expect him to change all his plans and come to a near-stranger for a religious experience. No. That was too far-fetched. I was just happy that he didn't make me feel like a half-wit for inviting him.

"Of course. I understand. I'm honored that you even gave it 5 minutes of thought."

I closed my eyes for one last time on the flight. The disquieting, yet ever-welcome sound of the landing wheels escaping from their womb stirred me from my momentary slumber. My ears popped. In a few minutes we would be on the ground. It had been a long, but pleasant flight. Soon I would reunite with my wife, my kids, and my own bed and pillow. That would be nice. And yet, a curious sense of urgency...no, not urgency...maybe determination brewed inside me. I just didn't want to say good-bye to Roni.

"Forgive me for being a pest, but when are you returning to Israel?"

"I'm actually going to be in the States for about 11 days," he said.

Outside the window, the cars no longer looked like toys and the baseball diamonds were adorned in January white. The mighty craft glanced the plowed and certain runway. Passengers applauded.

"Maybe you'd consider joining us for Shabbos NEXT week instead?"

I don't think I sounded desperate. I could be wrong, though. Roni shifted in his seat.

"I don't know," he said, *"but give me your phone number and if I can, I'll call you."*

I knew what that meant, but I scribbled my number on a napkin and handed it to him. We shook hands and parted.

Six hours later I was reveling in the aforementioned bed and pillow reunion. I was right — it was nice. The buzz of the intercom awoke me. It was my wife.

"Phone call on line 1...some guy named Roni..."

I don't recall having EVER jumped up so fast. This was no dream.

"Hello?"

"Hi! It's Roni...you know, from the plane."

"Yes, yes, yes...of course, of course...from the plane, from the plane."

I sounded like an idiot, I'm sure.

"Guess what," he said. *"You must have some connection upstairs. I'm at Port Authority, but all the bus routes to Montreal have been cancelled. It seems there is some kind of major ice storm there. I can't even get a flight out. So, I guess I'm coming to you for Shabbat. How do I get there?"*

This was not a Candid Camera stunt. About 45 minutes later the doorbell rang and in walked Roni. I just couldn't believe it. He actually came.

Over Shabbos we learned that despite the fact that he actually lived in Jerusalem proper, he had never — not even once — experienced Shabbos. We ate, we drank; we sang, we laughed; we prayed and we swapped stories. My kids found him totally charming and engaging. There was nothing anticlimactic about it. I guess you could say we had a grand ole time.

Here is the sad postscript. This story happened over seven years ago. From the moment he walked out of my door that Saturday night, we have never heard from Roni again. I think I took his number, but I misplaced it. I am embarrassed to say that I don't even remember his last name — it just didn't seem important at the time. It just felt like we were beginning a friendship that would last forever, but it didn't last at all...and I have no way of contacting him or even finding out who he was.

I'm a believer. And I believe that Roni may one day walk back into our lives. But meanwhile, I wait. And I ponder. How much did that one Shabbos mean to this mysterious guest? What ever happened to Roni? Does he still remember us like we remember him? Why wasn't I more responsible in securing his contact information? Does he ever wonder why we never tried to reach him? Did he lose my number too? Did he ever keep Shabbos again?

Opportunities lost; beautiful memories tainted with anguish and guilt. Roni, Roni, if you're out there...SHOOT us an email or a phone call. We'd love to hear from you.

The Possible Dream

*T*his is not a story about dreams.

Rather, it is a story about you. It is also a story about me. It is a story that happens to every single one of us and we don't even realize how real and how powerful it is.

My father passed away in 1986. He was 75; I was 34. To say that he was a gentle, humble and uncomplicated man would be understating the obvious. He didn't only epitomize those terms, he defined them. By trade, he cut diamonds; by profession, he loved his family. He had few friends, fewer hobbies, and loathed the limelight. He could sing and croon with the best of them, but try telling him that and the only response you'd get would be two flushed cheeks and a change of subject.

He raised a small family in Poland before the War, but they were murdered by the Nazis. I know almost nothing about them. Miraculously, he survived six years of concentration camp torment and came to America in 1947. Here, he remarried, had two sons, and dedicated his life to us. He never uttered the words "I love you." He didn't have to. He breathed them.

When he entered Mount Sinai for bypass surgery early Monday morning on March 24th of that year, he was nervous and wan. Nine hours later, after the surgical team bravely bypassed five clogged arteries, they wearily trudged into the waiting corridor and pronounced the operation a success. To have imagined that he would die there six months later, having never gone home again, would have been impossible. As the saying goes, *"The operation was a success, but the patient died."*

My mother, my brother, and I lovingly and dutifully did everything we could to will him back to health. Every single day we'd gather at his bedside — staring at monitors that we didn't understand, singing songs that we knew he loved, telling stories that we couldn't even tell if he heard — praying, hoping, rubbing, coaxing, grooming, practically forcing his eyelids open...but we never really had any reason to expect any improvement. It was so sad.

Then, one day, in early September, he woke up. Just like that. Suddenly he was coherent, lucid, and very much alive. The only ones more shocked than we were, were his doctors. I summoned all my children to the hospital and he spoke to each of them lovingly. We even discussed the distant possibility of his coming home. But like the flame of a candle that springs to life, flickering and crackling and dancing with implausible vigor seconds before it is stifled, Daddy fooled us all. Two days later he was gone. No warning. No premonition. Just the classical, morbid hospital phone call that shattered the usual morning scuttle, *"I'm sorry, your Dad died this morning."* Just like that. The ordeal was over.

I remember my eulogy. I cried my way through it, disjointed and mostly incomprehensible. Later I heard that friends were surprised at my overt and intense display of grief.

> *"The man was barely conscious for six long months,"* they reflected, *"why did he react like he wasn't expecting this? Was he in total denial?"*

Admittedly, it was a good question. But perhaps they hadn't heard about Daddy's sudden, but short-lived two-day recovery. Perhaps they had never personally experienced unconditional parental love. Or maybe they just didn't understand that death and mourning follow no rules.

And so I found myself, in the ensuing months, missing Daddy so very much. It wasn't easy. I wanted so much to see him again and feel his unspoken warmth and affection. Life went on, but something...something very special was missing.

It was more than a year later when I had *The Dream.*

In the dream it was winter; a Tuesday, I think. I was walking to my synagogue, just two blocks away, when I saw Daddy standing on the corner. He was alone. He looked wonderful. In real life he was short and stocky, but in the dream he looked almost tall. His white starched shirt gleamed in the brilliant sunshine and his large-knotted necktie protruded just a bit too much, as usual. He was wearing his favorite medium gray, double-breasted overcoat and his best and proudest smile.

I was a block away when I first saw him. Amid my elation at seeing him, I felt confused. Had he actually come back to visit me or perhaps he never died, after all? It never dawned upon me that this was only a dream. It couldn't be. The details were so sharp; the scene so perfect.

I started running toward him. He just waited at the corner for me to arrive. We hugged. I was so happy.

"Let's walk," he said.

We did.

He told me things were well with him, wherever he was, and that they allowed him to pay a quick visit with me.

"Where shall we walk to?" I asked.
"Let's go to the bank," he offered.

I was not surprised. The bank was one of Daddy's favorite places. He loved to go there. Not that he had any money, mind you. Maybe because of his mistrust of authority he felt he had to make sure the few dollars he had were still there — safe and sound. In those days, depositors held bank passbooks into which the teller would stamp your current account balance after adding in the interest that had accumulated since your last visit. He loved watching the pennies grow.

Daddy liked big banks, with very high ceilings, grand echoes, and elaborate architecture. And if the bank had a very secure sounding name, like *Manufacturers Hanover Trust Company,* that helped too. Clearly, he never would have put a dime in *Apple Bank.*

And so we walked to an enormous bank — probably the biggest I had ever seen, and took our place on a long line. Unlike most of us in the current ATM era, Daddy never minded waiting on line for things. It was part of his patient pace of life that we loved so much.

There was so much I wanted to tell him, and so I did. I just wanted him to be proud of the things I was doing. He listened. He nodded. He smiled. But after a few moments, he reached into his coat breast pocket and pulled out a newspaper. I was surprised, but only mildly. After all, Daddy loved reading the papers — Yiddish, English, daily, weekly — that was his chief relaxation after his day in the diamond district.

I wondered which paper he had with him and I asked. He turned it around so I could see it for myself. The headline read, *"Kol Yaakov (The Voice of Yaakov)."* I did not recognize it.

> *"What paper is that?" I inquired of him.*
> *"It's your paper," he said.*

He saw that I was puzzled, so he explained further.

> *"You see, where I am, they know that we want to keep track of what is happening to our loved ones. So, every day, this personalized newspaper, Kol Yaakov, is delivered to me. It is a full description of everything that you, Yaakov, are doing here on this Earth. I guess they know I like newspapers. So, you can tell me everything about yourself if you like, but, frankly, I really know it all already."*

Amazing. And yet, at the same time, it made so much sense.

I looked at Daddy with a blank kind of gaze, not sure what to say next. After all, whatever I could say he knew already. Daddy returned my vacant stare and then he patted me, ever so gently, on my left cheek. I could actually feel it. I could see he was proud.

And then he was gone. Again. No warning. No premonition. He simply vanished. I was left, standing alone, on line, at a cavernous and strange bank.

I awoke with a thud. I sat up in bed. Where had I been? The questions flooded my sudden and abrupt consciousness.

> *"Where's Daddy?"*
> *"If what I saw was real, why am I not at the bank?"*
> *"Was Daddy really alive?"*
> *"Perhaps his death was a dream?"*
> *"What time is it?"*

With the exception of the time (it was near dawn), I could answer none of the questions. The line between dream-state and reality was so blurred at that moment that I felt wedged into a kind of Twilight Zone. It was really weird. The cacophony lasted for several minutes.

Like a panic-stricken child drowning in untamed rapids, I felt myself frantically trying to grasp onto every minute detail I had just experienced. The images were slipping away fast. *"Maybe if I close my eyes really hard, I can go back to the bank and see Daddy again,"* I mused in quasi-desperation. But, of course, there was no going back. It took a few moments, sitting in the motionless shadows, but reality crept in — there was no place to go back to. It was all just a dream.

Crestfallen, I let my head slump to my somber pillow, as I stared at the useless ceiling above. The very first gesture of morning would soon beckon through my window. A new day was approaching. It would be a sad day. Not just another day without Daddy, but the day after I actually thought he was here, only to be awoken by the stark truth that the visit was only an illusion.

"A dream that has not been interpreted is like a letter that has not been read," says the Talmud.

I was familiar with the dictum of the Sages that the meaning and portent of a dream is influenced by the interpretation ascribed to it. It's hard to understand, but somehow, through some lofty process or course of action, the significance of every dream is very much dependent on how it is explained.

"But this dream needs no interpretation!" I argued days later. It contained no mystery, no unique or peculiar symbolism. Many, if not most dreams contain bizarre, or at least, far-fetched circumstances or scenes. Some even seem to foretell or warn of events that could be forthcoming. Not my dream. No. This was different. No Josephs need apply here. There was, it seemed to me, nothing in my dream that required any analysis or explanation of any kind. Daddy came, we embraced, we walked, we talked, he explained how he got all his information about me and he left. And it was beautiful.

And then it struck me. Perhaps it wasn't a dream after all. Maybe it really was a visit, albeit a nocturnal one. So what if I was asleep when it happened. The fact is, I really did see him. I heard him; I even *felt* him. By all definitions, there seemed to me to be no difference whatsoever between an *actual* visit and my *dream* visit!

Furthermore, the Talmud also states that there are three types of dreams that are destined to be fulfilled. And one of them is a dream that one sees in early morning, just before he wakes up. Maybe my dream — the dream of seeing Daddy just once more — was actually being fulfilled in the very dream itself.

A calm, inner peace descended over me. My conclusions made sense. Rather than feeling disappointment, I felt privileged…fortunate…perhaps honored. What I thought was only a frustrating illusion may just have been a most spectacular reality. The teaching of the Talmud was never more true — my own interpretation is what gave the dream its meaning.

All of us dream — at least we should. Some dream while awake, others while asleep. Sometimes we do both. But too often we paint the line between reality and imagination with a brush far too wide. And when we do that we make it that much harder to actualize our dreams, our potential. In truth, our state of reality and our fanciful imagination are really very close neighbors — residing side by side, in the same space — sometimes competing for our utmost attention.

Just another lesson that Daddy taught me.

"Dream away," I say. You might really build that castle in the sky.

Or a very large bank.

Touched by an Angel

I had seen him for years, but basically ignored him. I guess that's what many people do with kids who have Down syndrome. Ignore them. It's "easier" that way. They can be so unpredictable.

But this past Rosh Hashanah, all of that changed.

Moshe is almost 17. I'm no expert, but I suppose his retardation is moderate to severe. He's been coming to shul since he was 8 or 9. His mother brings him for the last 30-45 minutes of the Shabbos davening.

Moshe's routine has not changed dramatically in these last 8 years. He ambles in to the Sanctuary on his own and goes directly to his father. Dad greets him with a huge, welcoming smile, displaying no discomfort or embarrassment whatsoever. Sometimes he will sit; other times he stands. More often he paces.

Up the aisle, around the bend — sometimes stopping to stare at a random congregant for a few seconds — while other times his trip is the nonstop variety. On some days he visits the cantor at the front lectern or the rabbi; other times he skips them. No rhyme or reason, no destination. No apparent purpose.

Moshe rarely says anything either. His speech is rather garbled; his vocabulary limited. His favorite word seems to be "Amen," always recited a second or two after the congregational "Amen," and always two or three decibels louder than ours.

It is curious how little attention he garners. Most of my co-worshipers hardly seem to notice him. No stares, no questions, little, if any, interaction.

And Moshe does not *demand* our attention. Other than the occasional 3-second wordless stare, he just goes about his business. What exactly is that business? I have no idea.

I do wonder, though. In his darkened world of limited intellect, how much does he really comprehend? Does he recognize us from week to week? Does he feel the pain of his limitations? Does it matter if we smile and are friendly to him? Does his soul yearn for more?

Four years ago Moshe celebrated his Bar Mitzvah with a small gathering of family, faculty and schoolmates. Apparently, this event was quite meaningful to him — the Bar Mitzvah picture album is his constant synagogue companion. In between his wanderings, Moshe will sit quietly and methodically turn the pages of this most treasured tome. Over and over and over again. Flipping, staring, awkwardly adjusting his recently acquired eyeglasses and sometimes slowly running his fingers over the cherished photographs, as if never wanting to leave those joyous memories.

Then came Rosh Hashanah. For the last 22 years, I have had the awesome and humbling privilege of leading the congregational service. I am not a cantor by profession, but my shul, like many, prefers to employ regular members like myself to lead the davening instead of going the professional route. It is a responsibility I take very seriously and an honor I embrace.

This year was no different than most. My preparation, as usual, began many weeks before the holiday. My family and close friends know all the telltale signs. The most obvious one is hypochondriasis. The mysterious "tickle" in my throat, the Vitamin C and E that I ordinarily scoff at, and the garlic regimen make their annual appearance. My mood becomes a tad edgy and more serious.

Yet there was something a little bit different about this year. The world. The world is different. Al-Qaida, suicide bombings, anthrax, Saddam, a rash of kidnapings, reality TV, etc. The list is pretty extensive…depressing…and frightening. And then each one of us has his own personal anguish and tribulations to add to the list. No wonder the pre-Rosh Hashanah preparation period can be quite daunting — especially this year.

But sometimes a strange phenomenon occurs. The fear, the dread, and the pessimism can be so great and so awful, that instead of propelling us to greater reflection, change and prayer — the opposite takes place. We become inured...numb...almost indifferent. Thoughts like, *"What's the use? Nothing will change,"* and *"What's next?"* begin to creep in to our mind-set. Despondency rules. The feeling that we are just sitting ducks for the next misfortune or upheaval permeates our psyche. *System overload* cripples and overrides our inclination for inspiration and hope.

And that's what happened to me. Standing at the cantor's lectern, on the holiest day of the year, I found myself in this very spiritual funk. The day had arrived. No more time for preparation; no more garlic or introspection — just me, the *machzor,* hundreds of fellow congregants waiting to be led and inspired, and G-d. But something was wrong. I began the *Amidah* — the focal recitation of the day — and invoked the names of the *Avos* (Patriarchs), but something was missing. Something inside. Something deep. Something very important. *System overload* had taken my heart away.

"How could this happen?" I frantically wondered. *"Where is my compassion...my spirit...my soul? Where are my tears???"*

My lips kept moving and the words were still audible, but they were perfunctory, listless, detached, and alone. Never before had I been so keenly aware of my disconnected feelings and my desperate need to remedy my disengagement.

And then, things got worse. Enter Moshe. As if my mind wasn't distracted enough already, I looked up from my *machzor* only to find his silent stare just inches from my face. I felt like I had just driven over a six-inch pothole at 60 miles an hour. *"Now?"* I thought. *"My concentration is in deep enough trouble as it is. Can't he just visit the rabbi for a spell?"* I pondered callously.

Uncharacteristically, Moshe seemed to linger at the podium. He just stood there, looking at me. Expressionless. Seemingly, frozen in time and in no rush to continue his conventional stroll.

And then something happened. It's not easy to explain, but I think, for the first time, I *saw* Moshe. His gentility. His innocence. His soft hands and his silent eyes. I sensed Moshe's simplicity and wholesomeness. Here was a soul that was totally without sin, without blemish — the very definition of purity — right in our midst, just beside me, in fact. Staring at me, somehow silently communicating with me. My lips continued to perform, but my mind was now lost in this angelic emblem.

I felt my pulse quicken and my pupils widen. Suddenly I was riding the crest of an enormous spiritual wave, powered by the mere presence of a beacon of G-dliness.

Then without warning or fanfare, Moshe abruptly emerged from his momentary stupor. His eyes broke away from mine and fixed on the far end of the lectern. There, lying quietly and innocently, were a few stray tissues that I had placed as a usual precaution prior to beginning the service.

To my near amazement, I watched as Moshe looked at the tissues, looked back at me, and then carefully lifted one single tissue and tenderly placed it in the palm of my hand. It was the first real contact he had ever made with me. My prayers continued — they had to — but my mind was now far, far away. I looked at Moshe and firmly curled my fingers around my newfound gift. It was *only* a tissue, but at that moment...from that person...it was a precious symbol of the deepest understanding and care. The tears, only moments ago so distant, were suddenly unleashed.

It was then that I felt Moshe's warm touch as he reached out and tenderly began to stroke the very hand that completed his mission. It was soft and warm. It was comforting. He understood something about me and he wanted to help. One stroke...and then a second.

I peered through my newly blurred vision, hoping to catch a glance at the expression of my newfound friend, but he was gone. Having completed his calling, Moshe was already en route to some new unidentified pew. My now rejuvenated prayers, buoyed by the simplest of offerings, resounded with passion and reverence as never before. And for the next two hours, I never released that thin, fragile tissue from my grasp.

I made a new friend that day — a friend who I thought understood so very little about this world. And he reminded me of a wonderful expression I once heard about children like Moshe.

Some people come to this world to learn; others come to teach.

Heavenly Prayer

2 3K.

It's a window seat. It's my seat. Flight 012; El Al. The local time must be around 7 or 8 or 9 a.m. and, according to the map on my screen, we are somewhere between Halifax and Lisbon, I guess. It doesn't really matter.

I have just completed *Shacharis* (my morning prayers). Nothing unusual about that. It's something I've done every day for the past...er...many years. Of course, I'm usually 38,000 feet closer to the ground and in a shul when I *daven* (pray), but the words are very much the same.

I like prayer and I'll tell you why.

First of all, there's something special about speaking to G-d. It's a chance to check-in with my Manufacturer and get a sense of what, if any, repairs are necessary. Maybe all I need is an oil change or a new filter or a lube. Periodically a major tune-up is indicated. So it's good to stop in and open the hood.

Second, life today, as you know, is incredibly hectic. I needn't explain why. And prayer time is a preset regimen that allows for needed breaks from whatever it is we are engaged in. What a statement it is when we choose to begin and end our daily activities with a service of the heart and also find time in the middle of our day to do the same.

Third, I enjoy the shul. Men are directed to *daven* with a *minyan,* a quorum of ten, whenever possible and I take pleasure in the camaraderie and unity that the setting provides. My occasional visit to the pulpit to lead the service is a little bonus.

I wish it weren't so, but frankly, prayer is not always invigorating. It can become stale and hackneyed — bereft of meaning or purpose. In fact, it often does. Keeping one's prayers fresh and evocative, given the sheer frequency of this most holy pursuit, is a constant challenge faced by every man, woman, and child. There are no easy solutions.

But prayer on a 747, of course, presents a whole array of different challenges. Remembering to put your *siddur* in your carry-on, choosing the appropriate time and space to pray, when, whether, and how to stand, and (for men) donning the *tallis* and *tefillin* while crouched under an overhead bin are all complications and potential impediments to a meaningful and dynamic prayer experience. And depending on who your seatmate happens to be, you may have a little explaining to do when you're done.

But, like nearly everything in life, even these clouds of hardship in prayer contain silver linings.

As I return my *siddur* to the seat-pocket in front of me, I reflect on the prayers, just completed. And to my utter surprise, I am left with a good feeling.

Despite the aforementioned inconveniences, a strange, almost elevated, mood has wafted over me.

"Where did it come from?" I wonder.

Well, to begin with, Plane Prayer (PP) has two huge advantages over Synagogue Prayer (SP) — you can't come late and you can't leave early. How often are we seen huffing and puffing, even when praying at home, trying to catch the runaway *Shacharis* train or ducking out early to catch the runaway commuter train. With no fixed starting time and certainly nowhere to go when you're finished, PP affords you the rare opportunity to actually pray at any pace you like. It goes without saying that SP, with its power of a *tzibbur* (congregation), has other clear-cut advantages.

An added bonus to this most unusual experience is that you are not forced to "keep up" with the rest of the congregants or the *sh'liach tzibbur* (service leader). If you want to spend more time on a particular section, such as the *Shema* or the *Amidah*, you are free to do so.

And so I did.

I began by focusing some extra few moments on the oft attention-starved fifteen blessings that open the Morning Service. Our Sages teach that as one experiences the phenomena of the new day, he should bless G-d for providing them.

One example occurred when I came to blessing number 9 — *Blessed are You, Hashem, our G-d, King of the Universe, Who spreads out the earth upon the waters.* Had I ever stopped to contemplate an appreciation for G-d's having formed a hard crust over the planet's interior — made up of water, gases, and molten metals? Ordinarily, my eyes are still sealed shut and my lips are on cruise control until 20 to 30 percent of the service has passed.

Who doesn't take walking on a firm surface for granted? And who could have predicted that my gratitude for this newfound pleasure would multiply just 32 hours later, when I "survived" a 2-second earthquake in Jerusalem (really)?

Even before the blessings, I usually endow a full 25 seconds or so of SP to the holy song, *Adon Olam.* This short masterpiece, written over 900 years ago, succinctly proclaims G-d's attributes of being timeless, infinite, and omnipotent.

Today, however, during PP, I noticed that the author also included in the same song, the description, *"He is my G-d, my living Redeemer...He is my Banner..."*

I closed my eyes for just a moment and bask in the glow that an Omnipotent Creator is also *MY* G-d, *MY* Redeemer, and *MY* Banner. I loved the feeling of having a real and personal G-d — not easily discerned when driving 100 miles per hour during home praying or at SP.

Later, I let the engine idle while traveling through the *Baruch SheAmar* prayer. Commentators record an ancient tradition that this prayer was transcribed by the Men of the Great Assembly 2400 years ago from a script that actually fell from heaven!

And yet...usually...unfortunately...it hardly rates a reflection of any substance or even a second glance, I dare say. Today, however, I chanced upon the phrase therein that extols G-d, *Who Constantly Creates.* Today, it gave me pause. Creation was not limited to a one-time Big Banglike happening. No. G-d didn't just finish His project and go on vacation. Creation is ongoing...current...never-ending. And so are G-d's direction, guidance, and love. Something to remember.

Now regaling in the luxury of unhurried PP, I took a moment to consciously peer out my window. Usually, during home or SP, this activity is keenly discouraged; probably because the outside scenery on land would likely serve only as a distraction, not an enhancement of the prayer.

But today I wasn't drifting off; on the contrary, I was saying the verses:

> *It is You alone, Hashem, You have made the heavens, the most exalted heavens, and all their legions, the earth and everything upon it, the seas and everything in them, and You give them all life...*

Excitedly, I gazed out onto the horizon. The prophet was right. Having never flown in an airplane, he depicted, nonetheless, the magnificence of the celestial bodies, the expanse of the universe, the splendor of creation. I breathed deeply. I marveled at the commanding sunlight bouncing off the plane's fuselage, I winced at the robust wind currents that shook our craft, and I felt...oh...so small. Literally and figuratively, my prayers were carrying me to new heights.

I'm not sure if praying 7 miles higher than sea level really means the supplication is actually *closer* to G-d or not, but somehow I *felt* closer. Unperturbed by fellow congregants (who may occasionally *daven* too loud, out of sequence, or off key), crying babies, or telephones, unaffected by the boundaries of time, and impervious to all the usual distractions, I sat in my cabin of tranquility — just G-d, me and my prayer book. It was very special.

The illuminated seat-belt sign in front of me meant the *Amidah* ("standing" prayer)would be rendered a virtual oxymoron (I said it in my seat), but nothing could disturb this voyage of virtue. I just took my sweet time, reflecting on nearly every word — words that I had uttered tens of thousands of times but never really said...or understood properly.

And then I made a remarkable discovery. The word that is said more than any other, in the entire *Shemoneh Esrei*, is not *Baruch*, Blessed, or *Shalom*, Peace, or *Melech*, King, or even Hashem. It is the word *"attah"* — *You*: 33 times we refer to Hashem as *"You."* We speak *to* G-d. And we speak with great awe and reverence. And often, in the third person. But more often, we speak to G-d *directly.* We speak in the second person. We say, *"You!"*

Kings, queens, great rabbis, statesmen, even parents are, at times, referred to in the third person. It is a sign of ultimate respect. But the composers of our holy prayers, the Men of the Great Assembly — many of them bonafide, indisputable prophets — fashioned our most devout prayers in terminology that tells us to *converse* with G-d, freely, directly, comfortably, almost…informally. It is communication without hindrance, impediment, or veneer. Incredible!

Now inspired by the comforting thought that we are encouraged to see G-d as a Being we can easily relate to, I was reminded of a startling insight I once heard. One of the great mysteries of religious observance is the manner in which so many Jews sway back and forth during prayer. We call it *shukkeling*.

Tourists at the Western Wall, as well as less conversant observers of prayer in all locales, are often perplexed or even put-off by the seemingly strange calisthenics of enthusiastic Jews in intense prayer mode. But Rabbi Shimon Schwab, of blessed memory, offered a simple yet penetrating insight.

There are two primary vehicles for G-dly service — fear and love. Both are necessary components of a comprehensive and satisfying relationship with Him. Fear and love can perhaps be depicted by the manner in which we address Him. When we use the third person — *He*, *Him*, *His*, in the vernacular — it expresses awe, fear, reverence. Second person terminology — *You* — is a more casual and direct pronoun, perhaps portraying love. The swaying, or *shukkeling*, during prayer is an external manifestation of both properties — as we bend forward (expressing love) and draw away (demonstrating fear).

I gently pressed the button to recline 23K. I turned to the window once more. A momentary splash of turbulence stirred the weary travelers. For just a second, everyone was *shukkeling* — perhaps more in fear than in love. I smiled.

I gazed out at foreign terrain and alien bodies of water. Again, I felt small, but a good kind of small. Prayer can do that. PP was not something that I had looked forward to. All I had anticipated was how inconvenient and different it was going to be. Well…it was different.

In a few hours we would land in Israel. Soon thereafter I'll be praying again. I have a feeling it will be different too. All my newly gained insights will now be augmented by the sacred setting, enhanced by the Homeland, and stirred by the company of a *minyan* of like-minded Jews.

Of course, it will be different.

Plan B

*T*hose folks over at the entertainment industry sure do plan ahead, don't they? Today, they announced that one of their stars would be retiring...in 2009!

I heard right. You read right...2009.

I don't know about you, but I have trouble knowing what I'll eat for lunch today. Ask me where my graduates are going to school next year, and my stomach does a 360. Frankly, I'm not even sure what the next sentence of this article will be about! Last I checked, winter 2004 had just begun and they're already mapping out the fall 2009 schedule.

I'm not quite sure what to make of this. On the one hand, you have to admire this kind of advance preparation. As Benjamin Franklin put it, *"Look ahead or you'll find yourself behind."* Or, as our Sages taught us some 1600 years before Mr. Franklin, *"Who is wise? The one who anticipates the future"* (Babylonian Talmud, *Tamid* 32a). Makes a lot of sense.

On the other hand, we live in a world punctuated with uncertainty. Planning too far ahead often seems fruitless, even foolhardy. In business, politics, sports, the most confident predictions often turn out to be ludicrously wrong.

Perhaps G-d has something to say about all this. In fact, He does.

Rabbi Avraham Pam of blessed memory noted that G-d purposely allowed parts of His plan of Creation to require changes. He wanted to show us something.

On the first day of Creation, G-d said, *"Let there be light; and there was light"* (*Genesis* 1:3). But something was amiss. The Midrash explains that the light was of such spiritual intensity that G-d actually removed this light and "saved" it, so to speak, for the righteous in the World to Come.

On the third day of Creation, G-d created fruit trees with the unique characteristic that the bark of the tree would contain the same taste as its fruit (ibid. 1:11). Apparently, the earth had other ideas. The trees indeed produced fruit, but the bark did not *cooperate.*

Day four of Creation brought more imperfection. On that day G-d created two great orbs of light — the sun and the moon. The Talmud (*Chullin* 60b) explains that they were initially created equal in size. The moon, however, could not tolerate this sharing of the celestial throne and *complained* that "It is impossible for two kings to share the same crown." G-d responded by reducing the size of the moon. Again, change was necessary.

One might have expected a declaration of disappointment from G-d regarding these and other modifications. On the surface it seemed as if His plans had been challenged and even defied!

Quite the contrary — upon completion of the six days of Creation the verse tells us, *"And G-d saw all that He had made and it was very good"* (ibid. 1:31). Shocking. Despite the many shortcomings and alterations that accompanied the world's beginnings, G-d described it not merely as "good," but *"very* good."

G-d taught us a lesson of incalculable value. Just because our plans don't work out, that doesn't mean we have failed. You must be ready with Plan B. And Plan B can be "very good" too.

The fact that these "changes" took place in no way implies any imperfection in G-d or His Divine Plan. Nothing "surprises" G-d; that would be heresy. Perhaps G-d "planned" this Plan B process, so that we, his creations, can learn from it. Who are we to know G-d's ways?

We all like that feeling of being in control, even if it is often a mirage. We peer down the tracks or the boulevard to catch a hopeful glimpse of the approaching train or bus, as if our seeing it can will it to arrive faster. We delude ourselves, often within elaborate parameters, just to prolong the sometimes obvious fantasy that we are the true masters of our own destiny. It makes us feel comfortable, safe and snug. The notion that we don't really captain our own ship frightens us and forces us to flee into denial.

And over-preparation is a hallmark of that delusion. It is an exercise in futility and a statement about our slender belief system. We need to step back more often and allow the True Commander to chart the course. Of course we need to prepare and we need to do so responsibly. That is our charge. Without our full effort we are wrong to ask for or expect G-d's intervention on our behalf. But there's a fine line between doing our best and over-investing in our severely limited powers of preparation.

How often do we seek a particular item — a camera, a house, a gown — and after doing all our "research" and comparisons, we find that the one we really want is "no longer in stock," or discontinued, or not as good as expected. Sadly, many of us, when seeking a mate do the very same thing. We look, we compare, even do research…and then come up empty-handed. Over-preparation, in this case, takes the form of seeking perfection. Sometimes allowing Him to guide us means taking the plunge.

Often I am called upon to give a speech. It is usually a privilege, sometimes a thrill, but always a pressure. Many listeners are often surprised to learn that even well-known performers and seasoned speakers frequently experience a certain measure of anxiety before a presentation — no matter how comfortable they may seem to the public eye.

Early on in my speaking career, I was asked to address a rather large audience on a particularly esoteric topic. The closer I got to D-Day, the more I felt the tension mounting. And then I had a brainstorm. If I wrote out my entire speech, all 35 minutes of it — word for word — my angst would certainly be diminished. And so I did.

Well, my plan worked…to a degree. My nervousness was clearly reduced by knowing every word I would utter, but the reviewers basically panned the show. The overwhelming majority of listeners said I lacked passion and sincerity, and that I was "just not myself." They were right. My zeal had disappeared with my apprehension. It was the last time I tried that strategy. I had prepared too much and I paid the price.

Letting go isn't easy, even if we really do have faith in Him. But trust we must. And one of the best ways to amplify that trust is by reminding ourselves of what G-d has already done for us. Spend a few minutes a day taking an inventory of the everyday gifts and little miracles the A-mighty has provided for you. By reminding yourself of G-d's "proven record," you'll be boosting your capacity to let go. You'll find yourself preparing in a more reasonable way and relying on Plan B with confidence. And you'll stop fretting about Plans C, D and E.

Be cognizant of what it is you are preparing for. Evaluate each situation carefully before deciding whether to allow your "factory setting" to kick in or determining that this calls for less preparation than you are used to. Then get out of the way; demonstrate that your *real* trust is in G-d's hands.

Second, don't worry if have you have to rely on Plan B. G-d taught us in the six days of Creation that the result can be "very good" even if things did not work out as we had originally hoped.

Sure, 2009 is *right around the corner* for some people, but learning how to let go is a lifelong process.

Might as well start now.

You Can Stop
the Horror

*T*here are the victims. Their profiles vary.

One served falafel and chips for 12 hours a day on Rechov King George; another worked for the Wall Street Journal. One was a retired baker from Emanuel; another just began eating solids. One was a Bucharian Jew, struggling to find a new home; another was a 12-year-old boy of American descent, awaiting his Bar Mitzvah. One was a young mother vacationing at the Grand Canyon; another sold securities on the 96th floor of Tower #2. Their fate was, tragically, the same.

There are the perpetrators. Their profiles vary too.

One was from Fatah; another from the Tanzim. One was a cowardly sniper; another was a woman. One claimed allegiance to the Al-Aqsa Brigade; another waved the flag of Islamic Jihad. Their goal, tragically, was also the same.

And then there is us. You and me...and millions like us — the witnesses. Our experience over these past terror-filled 19 months does not vary very much. No matter where we live, we sit, glued to the media, afraid for our lives, and bewildered...totally bewildered. The questions never seem to cease.

"What was today's count?"

"Where did it happen?"

"How about the wounded?"

"When will this nightmare end?"

"What did Sharon say? Bush? Powell? CNN? Krauthammer? Friedman?"

"WHAT CAN WE DO?"

It's like we've been transported to a dreadful, evil planet, on loan from the demented mind-set of the creator of an old Superman comic book — where the prisoners have taken over. We feel like we're trapped in some kind of heinous *Groundhog Day* existence, spiraling in an abyss of helplessness and vulnerability. The faces may change, but the headlines stay the same.

DOESN'T ANYONE HAVE SOME ANSWERS?

And so, the saga continues. Pain, tragedy, grief...and more pain.

Maybe it is time to face a very difficult realization. And that is that the solutions we have tried, and those that we are most familiar and comfortable with, will never, ever, ever be successful. That means all the brilliant military, political, diplomatic and logical solutions to this perilous cycle of inhuman dread will never bring about its conclusion.

How much longer will it take us to accept this stark reality? How many more lives must be maimed or dismembered before we finally surrender our fantasies of resolution via mind or might? Sadly, we keep bringing our legendary stubbornness to new heights, with our most recent inflexibility of admitting our powerlessness to stop the Kamikaze mentality and strategy.

The truth hurts, but let's face it. Begin and Shamir couldn't solve the problem, and Rabin and Peres were no more successful. Netanyahu failed, so we tried Barak for a while. When his efforts proved futile, we turned to Sharon. Guess what? New faces — same results. Each one brought his own brand of guile and smarts to the table, but each one was turned back with blood on his hands and egg on his face. Harsh truths — but undeniable, nonetheless.

I look back on the months that have passed and I find just one single statement to have been completely on target regarding this tortuous conflict. It was a proclamation made by PM Sharon, after a flurry of deadly incidents a few months ago. He finally became convinced that Arafat could be officially declared "irrelevant." What he meant, of course, was that Arafat could no longer be considered a "player" in any future negotiation effort. He had "crossed the line," and was now deemed to be without portfolio or power. This was an accurate assessment, but not really "on target."

Inadvertently, however, Sharon had actually stumbled on the first truism of his political life. He was right. Arafat was, indeed, irrelevant. But not for the reasons he thought. Arafat was irrelevant because Arafat, in the greater scheme of things, *is irrelevant!* As a matter of fact, so is Sharon. He too is irrelevant! As is Bush, Cheney, Powell, Rice, Rumsfeld, Zinni and all the rest of the protagonists in this tragic real-life drama. They all don't really matter.

In fact, there are only two relevant *players* in this configuration — G-d and the Jewish People. That is it. Everyone else is just part of the cast. From Bush to bin Laden, and everyone in between. And like all good actors, they do *seem* to be very real; but they're not. As the wisest of all men, King Solomon, said*: "The heart of rulers is in the hands of G-d"* (*Proverbs* 21:1).

Naturally, there are heroes and villains and twists and subplots in this horror picture, but the plot and the characters are all creations of the infallible *Director* above. He writes, He produces, He casts and He directs. The production is called *"G-d and His People."* We may not like the circumstances very much, but it is about time we realized what this story is all about. The story is about us. And the amazing thing about this particular creation is that while most of the main characters are just messengers of G-d's will, we can actually...literally...change the script as it is being written.

I realize that this concept is probably not particularly new. In the back of our minds, we probably all reserve some space for the possibility that G-d truly runs the world; not kings, presidents, prime ministers, or terrorists. But the fact is that we are human...and we forget. We see the enemy blow up our neighbors and naturally, we are revolted, and filled with hate. We hear our leaders respond with rhetoric and ineptitude and we are frustrated beyond belief. We read the sage opinions of the great intellectuals of our holy periodicals and we reaffirm the drivel that Plan A or B might really solve the problem once and for all.

But the time has come to lift our spiritual cataracts. The only way this script is going to change is if we resolve to do something about it. And I'm not talking about Oslo, the Saudi plan, or all-out war. And if this sounds like some clarion call to Jews around the world to repent and make serious alterations in their lifestyles, well...that's exactly what this is.

Forgive me. If my plea for change smacks of any trace of *"holier than thou"* oratory, that is not my intention. But the situation is nothing short of desperate. If you don't believe that, just ask the surviving patrons of the *Moment* café in Rechavia or yesterday's bystanders on the bullet-riddled boardwalk in Netanya.

It can be no clearer than it is already. G-d is waiting, hoping, pleading, and screaming for His People to live the way they should. Simply put, each of us needs to bring more of G-d into our lives — in prayer, in trust, in charity, in the way we eat, talk, think, and relate to each other. The list is great, but the need is greater.

Truthfully, each one of us knows much of how we can improve our own lives. For some of us it lies in our dedication to teach others what we already know and understand, no matter how insignificant it may seem. For others, it is the commitment to learn more about what we should and should not be doing. Some of us are critically lacking in our relationship with G-d Himself; others need to acutely change the way they view their fellow men and women. Everyone must take stock of his own portfolio...and then begin the process of change.

But it is only when we stop vilifying our leaders, solely blaming our enemies, and worshiping the media...and begin to seriously look at *ourselves*, that this madness is really going to stop. Nothing else has, or will work.

The time has come.

The Restriction Prescription

*T*hey installed a water meter in my home. Just like that.

This calamity happened about a month ago. The doorbell rang. The man spoke with authority. He even had a clipboard with a dangling pen attached to it. "All your neighbors are gettin 'em too," he said. "It's the law!"

Ninety minutes later it was all over. The meter was installed. I didn't cry, but I wanted to. "Now they'll know exactly how much water I'm using," I moaned.

Life, as we knew it, would never be the same again. No more 40-minute showers. No more dripping faucets that I could ignore for months. No more endless water fights for my kids, with the driveway hose. Our long-standing, carefree lifestyle effectively came to an end on that fateful day.

A calamity? Indeed. But maybe it's more than just that.

Let's examine it from a very different angle. If we believe in G-d — a just G-d, a loving G-d, a compassionate G-d — then we also believe that G-d is only interested in providing for us, in giving to us. After all, if G-d is perfect, what could He possibly need or want from us? He has no needs or wants. Perfection, by definition, means that nothing at all is missing! And if there is really nothing that we can provide *for* G-d, what then is our purpose here?

It seems rather logical to me that if the only thing G-d "wants" is to give to us, our "job" is to find the best way possible to accept and utilize all the gifts He gives us, and to get the most out of all we receive!

What is G-d's method of giving us the maximum fulfillment of every one of life's pleasures? What recipe did He impart to us, that *guarantees* that we will enjoy and appreciate every avenue of satisfaction and happiness in this world?

In one word...restriction. In two words? Temporary restriction. Huh?

Surprising as it may seem, restriction is actually the single most important ingredient given to humankind that affords us the greatest opportunity to enjoy every positive experience on this planet.

For instance, I like steak. I like it very much. Rib, fillet, Sino, shoulder — you name it — especially if it is medium rare. But try having it every night. It's just not the same, is it?

Enjoy Bach? Shlomo Carlebach? Shwekey? Just try listening to them all day...every day.

What happens to your enjoyment level? Is it the same? Does it grow? Is that the premium method for experiencing the maximum amount of enjoyment from the steak? From Beethoven? From a roller coaster? A sunset? A vacation? A hockey game? A late morning nap? (O.K. Salomon, now you've gone too far.)

When G-d bestowed upon us that great instruction manual for living, also known as the Torah, he included in it 613 regulations, also known as mitzvos (commandments). These are the ingredients which, when adhered to, comprise that total recipe for fulfillment on this world. But only 248 of them are positive commandments — things to *do*. 365 of them are things *not* to do. O.K. — call them restrictions, if you like. Yes, symbolic of one each day, for every day in our solar year. And along with these instructions are a host of temporary restrictions that, when adhered to, comprise the greatest blueprint for our greatest enjoyment.

So valuable is this prescription that you'd be hard pressed to find ANY pleasure in this world that isn't lawfully proscribed, at least *temporarily*. Why? Not to punish us, restrict us, frustrate us or constrict our lifestyle. Quite the contrary! It is rather to make certain that we are pacing ourselves properly, so as not to overindulge on any single benefit this world has to offer — thereby diluting the excitement and appreciation of each experience.

Experiences potentially damaging to our bodies or souls are always prohibited — even though they might look enticing or like fun. Again, because it would interfere with our game plan of achieving lasting, maximum pleasure. But even the everyday stuff, which is given to us specifically to enjoy, is, at some time, made unavailable for us to experience. Of course, self-regulation could work too, but restrictive commandments are a lot more effective (and, therefore, more pleasurable). Suggesting to your kids that they *turn in early* for the next few nights to help them *catch up* on their sleep might not work quite as well as giving them a temporary curfew and sticking to it.

For example, not eating bread for a full eight days (Passover) may sound terribly oppressive to some. But anyone experiencing that "first slice of P.P.P. (Post-Passover Pizza)" knows how indescribably memorable it can be. It's a fresh appreciation of something to which we easily become habitually accustomed.

Numerous other examples come to mind. Music (during periods of personal or national mourning), creative work (Shabbos and holidays), comfortable shelter (Succos), eating (Yom Kippur and other fast days), telephones and computers (Shabbos) are some of the more obvious pleasures which are also temporarily restricted.

A really good parent knows all too well that the worst thing you can do to your child is to never say "No" to him. Want a sure-fire way to get him to hate that new set of hyper, ergo-dynamic, jumbo, turbo, energized, jet-powered, alpha-omega, quantum, phaser-propelled, prismatic Lego? Let him play with it ALL DAY...every day. Then watch his interest fade into cyberspace, or wherever things fade into these days. Life without restriction is colorless, jaded, and uninspired. Perhaps we are beginning to recognize that setting limits on the things we do only adds luster, passion, and vigor to the adventure we now call *life.com.*

Don't misunderstand me. I do not love my new water meter. But I suppose there is something to say for moderation, accountability, restriction and 8-minute showers.

Or am I just getting old?

"I Can't Wait for the Day When..."

*I*t's like I've always said, "I Love that International Herald Tribune."

The International Herald Tribune? Isn't that the newspaper that is wider than the aisles in Home Depot and thinner than the prospects for a lasting Mideast peace?

Isn't that the "throwaway" you ignore on the plane, in favor of...well...just about anything else?

The International Herald Tribune?

Yup.

There it was. Front page. December 19, 2000. An article that actually rouses the psyche and stimulates the spirit. (And inspires the theme for this piece, to boot.)

The premise is an absorbing one. Let's approach America's best and brightest young business execs, who are at the vanguard of our ever-changing universe, and ask them to complete the following sentence, "I can't wait for the day when..."

An intriguing assignment! Surely their responses will lend new insight into the mysterious phenomena that pervade our collective consciousness. What does Western culture *really* yearn for? What do our dreams say about our hopes for the future? Beneath the vacuous malaise that permeates our daily tabloids, cable channels, and websites, there must be an inner striving that tugs at our truest aspirations. What day can we not wait for???

Save the drum roll for some other occasion.

"I can't wait for the day when we have a cell phone that works everywhere in the world, one with one number that can be reached anywhere. That would be great."

So offers one young general manager from Southern California. That's the day he is waiting for. The day a cell phone works everywhere in the world. O.K. He's entitled, I guess.

"I can't wait for the distinction between the old economy and the new economy to disappear entirely," submits a 39-year-old managing partner of a growing venture capital firm. I wish I understood exactly what that meant, but I suspect you and I are better off being left in the dark on that one, anyway.

Of course, he too is entitled to wait for any day he wants to wait for — free country and all that. But I'm having some trouble relating very strongly to these dreams. Let's try another.

"I can't wait for the day when you hit the 'Submit' button on an Internet order and the UPS man is almost instantaneously on the porch."

I don't know about you, but I'm thrilled when I'm actually at home when the UPS man finally arrives. This executive vice president of a publishing company is seriously stating her life's dream as being **faster delivery service**? Am I missing something? Is that the kind of day *you* can't wait for? Has life really been reduced to cell phones, the new economy, and the instant UPS man?

Speed, of course, has become the going rage. It doesn't seem to matter much where we're going anymore, as long as we get there in a GIGA second. From dialing to dating, shipping to shopping, grilling, billing, surfing, banking…you name it! So, who can blame American executives for pining for the day when the future and the present practically coincide? Everyone gets caught up in the same web (pun intended).

I can hear the voices already. "He's another one of those old-fashioned, fuddy-duddy, anti-progress guys, yearning for the retro days when people actually heard busy signals and associated George

Foreman with boxing," you're probably saying about me. *Au contraire*, my friends. I loathe waiting for things just like you do. No sir. You won't catch me on a line at the post office or the Motor Vehicle Bureau these days. I'M TOO BUSY!

So progress, you see, is not my problem; nor is speed or convenience. They're all great. The only problem I have with this is the *"dream"* issue. There's nothing wrong with utilizing technological advances to improve our quality of life. Embracing our scientific explosion is wonderful. But should that really *dominate* our **dreams**?

The challenge of completing the sentence, "I can't wait for the day when…" is most compelling, indeed. In truth, it is a challenge that each one of us should confront in a most serious way. It is part and parcel of a course of action that Judaism calls *cheshbon*, or accountability. We are encouraged to "take stock" of our standing in every role of life that we play — and to do so on a regular basis. The essence of our daily prayers is actually this very same process.

Ask yourself:

> *"What kind of friend am I?"*
>
> *"Am I the best spouse/employee/parent/child/volunteer/ sibling/teacher I can be?"*
>
> *"What activities are really important to me?"*
>
> *"Do I surround myself with people who bring out the best in me?"*
>
> *"How do I spend my leisure time?"*

And then complete the sentence, "I can't wait for the day when…" Your completed sentence speaks volumes about your priorities in life. Of course, that sentence can, and perhaps should change frequently throughout your life. But when you know what it is you are waiting for, it helps you attain it more quickly and more completely.

But, hope abounds. Let us re-visit the *Tribune* for one final quote. This one from the chairman of a genomic company based in New Haven, Connecticut.

> *"I cannot wait for the development of drugs that would wipe out a number of deadly diseases…like cancer and late-onset diabetes. The hint of that reality is on us right now."*

Sounds like someone I'd like to have lunch with.

Now, you may be wondering how I would complete the same sentence.

So am I.

You see, how exactly you answer the question is not nearly as important as remembering to ask it.

Siyum HaShas: Pageantry With a Purpose

*T*he date: Elul 5720/early September, 1960.

The place: Zucker's Glenwild Hotel, New York's Catskill Mountains.

The occasion: Annual Convention, Zeirei Agudath Israel.

Hundreds of Zeirei youth, members and leaders, clamor and strain to catch a glimpse of Hagaon Rav Aharon Kotler, of blessed memory, as he approaches the microphone to address the gathering. The overflow crowd, whose numbers defy the yellowed maximum occupancy sign on the wall, rise as one in reverence for the eminent *gadol*.

The Rosh Yeshivah speaks: "I am going to begin by making a *Siyum HaShas* (completion of the Talmud). For today is the day of the fifth *siyum* for those who have been learning Daf HaYomi (one folio per day for seven-plus years)." The *gaon* completes *Mesechta Niddah* and says the *Hadran* (closing prayer). No one joins in. No one else is sharing in this propitious occasion.

The scene shifts. It is now nearly 29 years later.

The date: Rosh Chodesh Iyar 5750/April 26, 1990.

The place: Madison Square Garden, Main Arena, New York City.

The occasion: Ninth *Siyum HaShas* of Daf Yomi.

Twenty thousand men, women and children, representing every walk of Torah Jewry, assemble under one roof for the loudest proclamation of allegiance to Torah study in United States history. Forty thousand eyes witness the strength and unity of Torah, reminiscent, perhaps in some small way, of Sinai itself, while 40,000 ears hear a thunderous *"Amen, Yehei Shemei rabbah mevarach..."* that will echo *in their hearts forever!* *Yes. We have come a long way. Baruch Hashem.*

ᦉ PERSPECTIVE

Shlomo HaMelech taught us the appropriate vehicle for *kiddush Hashem: "B'rov am hadras melech* — In the multitude of people is the King's honor" (*Proverbs* 14:28). Too often, in our recent past, Jews in vast numbers have found themselves congregated for events hardly noted for their joy or celebration; i.e., funerals of *gedolim*, mass protests, and the waiting rooms of genocide. Millions of human sacrifices, Torah giants among them, journeyed on trains to extinction — never to see their families again, never to cherish Torah or even taste its beauty once more.

But on April 26th 1990, not fifty years later, the subway trains will stop at 34th Street in Manhattan, and some of those same passengers, along with thousands of their children, grandchildren and *chaveirim* will surge forth from the exits and join in an unparalleled demonstration of sanctity and harmony.

Of course, the ushers and ticket-takers of Madison Square Garden are not exactly strangers to sell-out crowds. SRO (standing room only) events have been ho-hum for the folks at Gulf & Western for decades. Only this time, the protagonists will not be names like Frazier, Esposito, or Sammartino. Rock artists and lion tamers will not be in attendance. In their stead, *maggidei shiur*, prominent rabbanim, Chassidic leaders, and leading roshei yeshivah will shine in center stage. And the usual cheering and jeering of the crowd will be replaced by the uniform urgings of *"Hadran alach Shishah Sidrei Mishnah u'Gemara,"* and *"Hashem yevarech es amo bashalom."* Indeed, as the nightmare of one generation unfolds into the dream of another, the fulfillment of the *navi* Zechariah's prophecy is a poignant reminder of the pre-Messianic era in which we live. As interpreted by our *Chazal:* "Theaters and circuses are destined to be converted into synagogues and halls of Torah study (*Megillah* 6a) — if only for one day, this time celebrating the completion of the entire Talmud, one *daf* (two sides of the page) at a time, following the pioneering course charted by Rabbi Meir Shapiro, of blessed memory, the Lubliner Rav, in 1924.

∞ "WE ARISE AND THEY ARISE"

And so the *Shas* will be completed and the traditional *siyum tefillos* will fill the arena! *"Annu mashkimim v'hem mashkimim — We arise and they arise. Annu mashkimim l'divrei Torah, v'heim mashkimim l'dvorim beteilim — We arise for the words of Torah, they arise for insignificant frivolity."* Directly above, championship banners and retired uniforms of sports heroes of yesteryear will hang from the Garden rafters and remind us of our exclusive status as the *"mamleches kohanim v'goi kadosh."* Let us pray that we will be worthy.

And then *Kaddish* will be said. The special *Kaddish*. The *Kaddish* reserved only for a *siyum*...and a burial. The *Kaddish* that will leave no eye dry, as the memories of six million *kedoshim* will be evoked and sanctified.

But even tears of anguish must also contain tears of joy. For this special *Kaddish* bears a special commonality in its recital at a *siyum* and a burial. Both of the moments only appear to be endings. They are, in fact, beginnings. Termination of one's life on this world is actually the beginning of one's eternal existence. And the culmination of the entire Talmud is also the start of the tenth cycle of Daf HaYomi, bringing new hope and the opportunity of fulfilling in some small way the dreams and the promises for greatness that were so cruelly crushed a half-century ago.

Repairing Hashem's Family
Making Israel's Pain Our Own

I suppose we all should feel just a tad embarrassed.

Do we *really* need an article about how to feel the pain of our brothers and sisters in Israel? Is it necessary for us to develop strategies, create initiatives, and plan activities that can ensure that the interminable terror that our compatriots in *Eretz HaKedoshah* (the Holy Land) experience constantly remains foremost in the Diasporan collective psyche? Shouldn't this kind of empathy be automatic? Instinctive? A natural reaction for the *Chosen People?*

And if we are not embarrassed, shouldn't we at least be embarrassed about that?

And yet, such is the case.

Some years ago, Rav Chaim Mintz, of the Yeshivah of Staten Island, had left his wristwatch somewhere and was rushing to another location. Uncharacteristically, he asked a student if he wouldn't mind retrieving it for him. "I wouldn't trouble you if I wasn't so short on time," he explained.

The student was all too willing to fulfill the simple mission.

Upon his return, the student questioned his rebbi. "Excuse me for prying," he said, "but I couldn't help noticing that the rebbi's watch has the incorrect time even though it seems to be working," he pondered. "Shall I adjust it?"

"No, no," replied Rav Mintz. "You see, the time on my watch is actually precisely 7 hours ahead of New York City time. I always keep it set to Israeli time so I can keep a constant reminder for myself about the situation in Israel."

It seems that **years** before, there had been a terrorist attack in Jerusalem. Many lives were lost and Rav Mintz wanted to be certain he never forgot it.

No. Keeping them in mind is not necessarily automatic.

A personal story...

It happened about a year and a half ago. It was a Tuesday night, I believe, and I had just finished davening Maariv (evening service) at Rabbi Landau's well-known Beis Midrash in Flatbush. It was about 10 p.m.

On my way out, a note, posted on the lobby wall, caught my eye. It read:

"Shmuel G. is sitting shivah at _____. His wife was the only American fatality in the Sbarro's bombing in Jerusalem."

My friend, Shimon, read the note along with me. Neither of us recognized the name. Both of us exited in silence. How tragic.

I joined Shimon for the short ride home. As I bid him goodnight, he asked me, "So, when shall I pick you up?"

"Pick me up for what?" I responded. (I was unaware of any previously made plans.)

"Well, for the shivah, of course," came the reply.

"The shivah?" I pondered innocently, "I don't really know the fellow and hadn't planned to go. Do you know him?"

*"No," he said, "but how can we **not** go?"*

Never had a lump appeared so quickly in my larynx. It was the lump of shame. The contrast was oh, so clear...and painful. To Shimon, visiting and consoling this grieving survivor was instinctively proper and thoroughly obvious — his unfamiliarity notwithstanding. To me, it was never even a consideration. Why would I visit someone I don't know?

But the story does not end there. Lesson learned, I asked Shimon to pick me up at 9 a.m. the next morning. He did. We

*arrived at the mourner's home and awkwardly ventured in. In
a feeble attempt at repentance, I led the way. To my surprise,
the mourner greeted me immediately.*

"Yaakov Salomon, so nice of you to come."

*I recognized Shmuel immediately as a Shabbos guest of
the past, who had graced our table several times. His name
had eluded my memory. Shmuel then turned his attention to
Shimon, our hero, and asked, "And who are you?"*

*We sat down — me, with my oversized lump; Shimon,
with studied compassion. People trickled in. And as each
one arrived, he was greeted by Shmuel with the same refrain,
"And who are you? Did you know my wife?"*

*Within 10 minutes or so, we were joined by about a dozen
people. In a display of startling irony, the only person whom
Shmuel knew in that room was me! The rest were, like
Shimon, just wonderful compassionate Jews — demonstrating their kinship and concern. Mi ke'amcha Yisrael ([G-d],
who is like Your nation, Israel)?*

So, perhaps many of us DO feel their pain, but many of us…
including myself…seem to be lacking.

∽ WE ARE NOT HELPLESS…

Some may argue that *remembering* their travails and their pain
doesn't accomplish very much. *"They don't need us to cry for
them,"* goes the refrain, *"they need the madness — the terror, the
funerals, and the grief — to STOP."*

But might that not be precisely the point? Is it so far-fetched to
posit that the crying we do for them, and the resulting prayers that
are sure to emerge, may just be the solution as well? Couldn't the
simple manifestation of our genuine concern be the precise unwrit-
ten prescription to cure this ghastly decree?

Sadly, our current predicament is hardly unfamiliar to us. Our
storied history is sated with tribulations that seem to always threat-
en our very existence. *"Z'chor yemos olam,"* the Torah implores.
We must "keep our eyes on our history." There is much to learn.
Guidance may be lurking in those yellowed pages.

R' Elchonon Wasserman, in his classic *Kovetz Maamarim*, provides some of that guidance. He classifies the perils which we have

constantly confronted, into two categories — threats to our physical existence (such as the Purim saga) and threats to our spiritual existence (as in the Chanukah era). And our responses to those dangers must serve as guideposts for all of time.

"Threats to our spiritual survival," writes Reb Elchonon, "are best met by our willingness to take military action. This is best exemplified by our battles, and improbable ensuing victories against the *Yevanim* (Syrian-Greeks). And the frightening specters of physical annihilation must be answered by clarion calls of *teshuvah, tefillah,* and *tzedakah* (repentance, prayer and charity). Nowhere in *Megillas Esther* is the notion of a military campaign against Haman suggested.

And so, I humbly offer the suggestions that follow. With over 700 holy souls gone to date, and many thousands more crippled and injured — both physically and emotionally — the illogicality of a military solution should, by now, be painfully obvious. So the proposals presented here have a decided spiritual bent — with an inclination toward the concept that **truly** feeling their pain, and showing it, may be a road to resolution — not just to compassion.

The exhortation by our Torah leaders to daily recite specific chapters of *Tehillim* (*Psalms* 83, 130, 142) should, of course, be a given for every caring Jew. *Tehillim* has, is, and always will be our first mode of action in times of crisis.

∽ BUT WHAT ELSE CAN WE DO?

Participants in any worthwhile endeavor are usually sorted into three basic groups — beginners, intermediates, and advanced. So let us offer a specific intervention for each category (with the secret hope that everyone will want to consider himself "advanced," and thereby embrace all three suggestions).

If you see yourself as a beginner, don't feel bad. I assure you, if nothing else, that you may well be more realistic than those who place themselves in the other categories. At least you want to start.

You need something as a daily reminder, besides the demoralizing news reports and accompanying grisly photos. And what better daily reminder than our daily prayers? Consider, if you will, the following little-known opinion in Jewish law.

The *Rama* (*Orach Chaim* 113:1) explains that we are not free to bow down wherever we desire in *Shemoneh Esrei* (the *Amidah* prayer). Bowing is permissible only in the specific places decreed by the Sages. But the *Mishnah Berurah* (written by the saintly Chofetz Chaim), quoting the *Maharil,* opines that we should bow down at the beginning or the end of the blessing of *V'lirushalayim ircha.* And the *Magen Avraham* adds that perhaps a slight deferential bowing would be appropriate.

We don't rule like the *Maharil.* Fine. We needn't follow the *Magen Avraham.* Well enough. But here we have a highly respected halachic authority "suggesting" that we bow down during the blessing of *V'lirushalayim ircha!* None of the other twelve blessings of the middle section of *Shemoneh Esrei* appears to qualify for that special consideration. Doesn't that mean **something**? Shouldn't that propel us to have at least *a bit extra focus* during that blessing? Prostration? Maybe not. But concentration? Definitely! At the very least, it guarantees that we think of them three times a day. A perfect start for every beginner.

As for the intermediate grouping, extra *focus* during the blessing for Jerusalem should also be a given, but why not make a beginning attempt at a marvelous and most compassionate movement to get every synagogue in America to "adopt" an Israeli family who has suffered a recent loss in the reign of terror.

Besides the tremendous reward involved, I can guarantee, psychologically, that adopting a grieving family as part of your own is nothing short of a magical formula for setting your life's priorities in proper order. And the message it communicates to your children is one that could never be taught in a classroom or communicated from a book. Can you think of a more important goal? I can't.

And at last we turn to the advanced group.

It is you who owns a true appreciation and a deep respect for the hundreds of thousands of families for whom, every day, terror has become an overwhelming feature of everyday life.

You understand that it is not only important and proper to make **their** pain **your** pain, but you have an inkling...a conviction, that feeling their anguish and their grief could actually be a significant ingredient in the formula for helping it vanish.

You have grown tired of listening to the news, and weary of worn-out and hackneyed military, political, or strategic solutions that have never worked and never will.

You don't doubt that, painful as it is to admit, G-d is sending **all of us** a harsh, horrific and glaring message that something is very wrong in our camp. And that His very specially selected family needs a major spiritual overhaul.

Needless to say, I am certainly not privy to His incomprehensible workings. But one observation, if you will permit.

∽ THE AT-RISK CONNECTION...

Our communities, here and abroad, have, for the past years, been suffering with another overwhelmingly excruciating crisis. It is the one that has been termed "Kids at Risk" — the shocking and agonizing process of watching some of our most talented and engaging youngsters abandon the way of our ancestors, for the scourge of aberrant behaviors. And while much is being done to attempt to ameliorate the situation, the battle rages on. It is still very very painful.

And we wonder, and maybe we always will wonder, why do kids leave the straight path? Why do they veer from a life that can bring them enormous satisfaction? Why do great kids from good, loving families reject nearly everything they are taught? And why do we suffer from this devastating malady, more than any previous generation?

Perhaps...just maybe...G-d wants **us** to feel *His* pain, so to speak. Let us for a moment compare His family with our families — in the "at-risk" category.

No one can minimize the heartbreaking and tragic pain of watching, or living with, a youngster on the fringe. Each and every soul is so very dear and cherished. But despite the disheartening at-risk numbers, it is somehow infrequent that more than one child per family suffers from this terrible condition. The collective family pain of having even one such child seems almost too much to bear. It does happen, but it is uncommon.

But G-d *also* has a family. He is *Avinu Malkeinu, our Father, Our King,* and we are His children. Let's look at **His** family. How are THEY doing? Not *nearly* as well as our families. You see, in His family, it's not one child who is off the path. He doesn't have two children who are at-risk. In G-d's family nine out of ten of his children do not know how to say the *Shema*, have never shaken a *lulav*, have never braided a challah, and have never heard of the Chofetz Chaim!

Let the numbers startle you! Nine out of ten of HIS children are lost due to apathy, ignorance, intermarriage and assimilation…and the numbers grow as you read this.

Be honest. Do we feel *His* pain? And could the agony and anguish that we experience with our at-risk kids be a message to **us** to feel **His** pain?

Imagine for just a moment (more than that would be too painful for us). How would one of us actually feel if nine out of ten of OUR children **knew nothing about Jewish life?** Would we just choose to focus on the positive?

> *"Oh, at least I have one child who keeps the Shabbos, learns a little of Torah, married Jewish — thank G-d for that. The other nine? Well, what can you do? At least we tried. I guess you can't win them all. Pass the pretzels please."*

Or, more than likely, would we totally fall apart from grief and heartbreak and never sleep well again?

Maybe, only maybe, G-d feels that we need to experience at least a fraction of that heartbreak.

But if that is so, or even if it's only partially true, then the *kiruv* efforts of this advanced group can be a resounding message to our Father that we DO care about the family, after all. And that it is NOT acceptable to us that 90 percent of our family members never said a blessing in their entire lives and define their Jewishness by opposing prayer in public schools and voting (or not voting) for Joe Lieberman.

And similarly, when we experience over 29 months of constant terror, and we know that our response must be a spiritual one, then the *kiruv* efforts of this group can announce to G-d that there IS unity among His children. And yes we TRULY **do** care about **every single Jew** — even those that seem so different from us, or so far from us.

Is that *really* what G-d is truly waiting for? I don't know. Perhaps no one knows. But if 90 percent of **YOUR** family had drifted away, what would YOU want to see?

The Heavenly Report Card

*O*ur lives on this planet seem to be totally results oriented. No matter how hard your tailor tries, if he doesn't finish the suit on time he doesn't get paid. We don't reward him with 80 percent of his payment if the jacket is *only* missing one sleeve. The suit is useless without it. He gets nothing. And that is reasonable.

But on the *Heavenly Report Card* the grading system is very different. Our Sages teach us that the relative success of our endeavors is not really in our hands. Surely we must put in our fullest efforts in any task we undertake, but what ultimately transpires is beyond our control. How often are we faced with a situation where despite our most heroic and skilled labors, the end result falls far short of our expectations? Conversely, sometimes things just seem to "work out" *despite* our paltry investment.

"Ben Hei Hei says: The reward is in proportion to the exertion" (*Ethics of the Fathers* 5:26).

G-d, in His infinite wisdom, gave us free will — the ultimate gift. And in doing so, He designed a system whereby he could reward us *strictly* for trying. The results are totally up to Him.

Upstairs, we are *never* judged by the end product, only by our intentions and our corresponding effort toward fulfilling our objectives. When we do that, we are 100 percent successful — regardless of the outcome.

Life's greatest insights come in all shapes and surprises. Often they are packaged in profound experiences and dramatic episodes. But sometimes they are delivered in simple little packages — containing reminders of things we all know, but too often forget. I have Daniel and Sharon to thank for this one.

Daniel and Sharon are devoted and loving parents. To them, raising children is much more than a filial obligation or a playful recreation. It is a calling.

When I first met them they were married for six years and already had four children. Daniel had built a small but thriving consulting business while Sharon spent 24/7 consulting with bottles, pacifiers, and nurseries.

They had sought my counsel regarding Ari, age 5. He seemed to be moody at home with a penchant for tormenting his sisters, and his teacher had used the word *reclusive* in describing Ari at a parent/teacher conference.

Daniel and Sharon were overwhelmed, but at least they realized it. They pulled no punches. They came with prepared questions and freely confessed to their helplessness with Ari.

"Don't ask me how a 42-pound 5-year-old can completely take over a family of six, but it has happened. I've seen it," cried Daniel.

The details are not especially relevant. Suffice it to say that we spent five subsequent appointments discussing some management strategies for dealing with Ari. At a three month follow-up session the parents reported some very minor improvements in Ari and only slightly more substantial progress in their own coping skills.

It was 12 years before we met in person again.

"Let me guess," I said when they called. "Ari turned 17."

Daniel wore an enormous yet artificial smile as he entered the office but Sharon's tension could not be masked. I barely had time to ask, "How are you guys doing?," when Sharon dropped her purse on the floor and blurted, "We are losing our son."

Daniel and Sharon then proceeded, taking turns spilling out the specifics of Ari's swift and steady decline into a world of confusion. I was doing little to interrupt their venting voyage; just letting them unleash some of the agony was probably more valuable than any great wisdom I could offer them.

Ari never did better than 'C' work, usually worse than that, despite his obvious intellectual capacities. Only in seventh grade, under the tutelage of an exceptionally dynamic rebbi, did Ari display any real motivation to learn.

"He was so happy that year," recalled Daniel. "He had friends; he had a spark — he laughed. We thought we had turned the corner."

"But after his Bar Mitzvah," continued Sharon, "everything went south. We tried to get him to see someone, but he refused. He wouldn't see you because he knew we had spoken to you about him. You were off-limits — but so was anyone else. He never said why."

Over the next few sessions I learned that Ari had become exceedingly withdrawn in high school. He vacillated between religious fanaticism and total secularism. He would often just seem to drift into his own world, displaying very occasional fits of anger that manifested his deep underlying frustration with himself and his situation.

All the while Ari continued to attend school, but he developed obsessive-compulsive symptoms that sometimes included bizarre rituals of excessive cleanliness. His grades even improved, but socially he was inappropriate and he certainly was unhappy.

I remarked how tragic the situation was, especially since it was so clear that therapy and medication would likely have helped him — but he just wouldn't hear of it.

Daniel and Sharon continued to come on a weekly basis for a while, detailing the heartbreaking odyssey that had unfolded before them.

"The pain has been unbearable," said Daniel, "but at least it never divided Sharon and me. If anything, it has made us closer. And ironically, maybe *because* of Ari, we have put so much more into the other kids. Thank G-d, they're all doing great."

Hard as I tried, there was simply no idea that I came up with in the ensuing weeks that they hadn't already attempted. They wrote him letters. They stayed up nights, both with him and with each other, trying to find some common ground to relate mutually with Ari. His grandparents pleaded with Ari to get help — to no avail. His teachers attempted to engage him. Neighborhood rabbis, even Kabbalists, prayed for him. Nothing worked.

She buried her face in her hands and the tears flowed shamelessly.

"I'm a failure."

I could see that Sharon had reached the breaking point. I just let her cry; partly because she so *needed* to and partly because I really had nothing to say to her. My only lame intervention was gently pushing my box of Kleenex closer to her.

Many minutes went by without a word being said. The ticking of my fake grandfather clock never sounded so loud.

Sharon finally looked up at me and wiped away her final tear. Her tired eyes seemed to beg me to say something...anything...that might remotely soothe her.

"I know you feel like a failure and that the pain you are in may never ever go away. The hurt is beyond description.

"All I can say to you is that as long as I have known you, you have been an incredible parent. Raising your children properly was and will always be your number one priority. That is something to be very proud of.

"But success in parenting, like in most things, is really not measured by how your kids turn out. That's a mistake. It's a mistake that many parents make. But we both know kids who happened to turn out great *despite* having parents who couldn't care less about them. That's just the way it is. We don't really understand why.

"A great rabbi once reminded me that true success in life is measured *only* by how much effort you put in. You're no failure. Frankly, Sharon, in my book, you are 100 percent successful. We all hope things will turn around, but regardless of what Ari does with his life, you and Daniel could not have been more successful. You have done everything you possibly could and more. You are both champion parents."

The quiet returned to the room. I wasn't sure if my impassioned remarks hit home or not. Sharon looked at the floor and then at me. I thought I saw her smile.

"Thank you," she finally said.

"Thank you so very much. I feel like I have waited 17 years to hear the words that you just told me."

∽ A COMPLETE SUCCESS

We parents need to remember that we're judged by our sincere efforts, not the results. Don't get caught up in the mundane Earthly marking system. When you do your best to raise your kids with solid values, unremitting love, and sensible discipline, while also being an appropriate role model for them to emulate — you are automatically a *complete* success — no matter how they respond. It isn't easy to keep that focus, but it can save you barrels of frustration, disappointment, and guilt.

The same dynamic actually holds true in countless areas of life. As long as you're doing your *absolute best*, whether it's trying to raise money for a really important project, learning subjects that seem out of reach, attempting to close a mega-deal, baking a cake or just choosing a cool tie — you can and should consider your efforts *totally* successful. It's hard, but don't be misled by the outcome.

What the future holds for Ari I cannot say.

And Daniel and Sharon surely have some tough challenges ahead. They may still experience pain, frustration, and disappointment. No one can really know why.

Hopefully, though, *failure* is no longer in the picture.

Can't Sleep?
Why Not?

*T*his is a story about insomnia, filmmaking, and Rosh Hashanah. If you don't think they're related to each other, read on.

Insomnia, in this country alone, is rampant. Check out these staggering numbers.

A quick Google search on insomnia yields 3,690,000 links in 0.28 seconds.

Thirty million Americans suffer from sleeplessness regularly.

Direct costs of treatment are conservatively estimated at $14 billion.

It seems that a lot of people, in a lot of bedrooms, in a lot of cities have some serious trouble falling asleep at night — and they're not very happy about it. *You* might even be among them.

Insomniacs will try almost anything to get a few winks: pills, herbs, therapy, hypnosis, wine, mind games, calcium, a really boring book, white noise, warm milk (I'd rather be awake all night), talk radio, counting sheep, learning, audio tapes, hot baths, sleep clinics…you name it, they've tried it.

But even if you're not a chronic insomniac, surely you've had experience with this rather unpleasant phenomenon now and then. Fun, it isn't.

Which brings us to filmmaking (don't worry, we'll get back to insomnia soon). I recently returned from Israel, where I was involved in the filming of a soon to be released major documentary, titled *"Inspired!"* The film tells the engrossing tale of what motivated so many people in the last few decades to eschew a secular lifestyle and discover Torah, discover meaning, discover purpose.

I met dozens of fascinating people — journalists, teachers, students, accountants, rabbis, housewives, psychologists — people from every walk of life who continue their career of choice but with more spirituality, more enthusiasm, and more clarity than ever before. Basically they told their stories into the camera, one more captivating than the next, and explained why they did what they did.

And while each personality certainly made an impression on everyone on the set, there was one man...one moment, actually... that stood out for me. It was a declaration made that I will not soon forget — a sound bite that will probably, no, *hopefully*, reverberate inside me forever. Curiously, the statement this man made was not especially profound nor was it particularly insightful. Its impact lay in its simplicity and its sincerity.

Some of you recent history buffs may recognize the name Eliyahu Essas. Now in his early 60's and living in Jerusalem, Essas made his mark in the pre-Glasnost era of the early 70's. Growing up in the atheist tundra of Central Russia, he discovered G-d through independent reading and went on to teach and inspire scores of zealous disciples, and spearheaded the entire Refusenik movement.

Repeatedly confounding the KGB and literally risking his life with every verse he taught and every candle he lit, Essas crawled through the crevice that formed when the Iron Curtain cracked, and today he continues to shine a light for curious Soviet Jews around the globe who seek his wisdom, direction and advice.

We were about 20 minutes into the interview. The Jerusalem sun was baking the equipment, the crew and Essas himself. With a curious combination of charisma and humility, Essas was espousing his staunch belief that every Jew in the world who experiences the beauty of his religion has a duty to share that splendor with those not yet exposed to it.

And then, without a word of warning, he said it. With a vocabulary as pronounced as his accent, he leaned forward to speak, as if beckoning the camera to come in close. It did.

"I know this may sound like an exaggeration or it may even sound boastful, but I must tell the truth."

My ears perked up.

"There are many nights, still today, when I literally cannot sleep because I am so worried about the future of the Jewish People."

The interview came to a sudden halt. An odd silence came over the set. This man **meant it** and all of us knew it. Easily and immediately, I imagined him tossing and turning...racked with turmoil and uncertainty...at 3 or 4 a.m....because the fate of the Jewish People is so precarious. Incredible.

Which now brings us to Rosh Hashanah. Rosh Hashanah is many things to many people, but primarily it is the beginning of the ten-day period of judgment for all of us. In addition to all the special prayers, greetings, blessings and the shofar blasts that herald in this awesome annual juncture, our Sages, long ago, advised us against napping on the day of Rosh Hashanah. *How can one sincerely present himself before the Creator and appeal for Life itself while still finding the opportunity to steal away for a little siesta in the afternoon?*

Apparently, standing in judgment while also having the ability to wile away a few hours in slumber do not sit in great congruence with each other. When you really care about something, when a situation *really* bothers you, your capacity to fall asleep must naturally be impaired — if not, then what you *think* is bothering you may not be as important as you thought it was.

Self-realization, the power of true and complete honesty with one's goals, motivations, strengths and weaknesses, is the most powerful tool in the world for self-actualization in *anything* you endeavor to accomplish. This is the lesson of Eliyahu Essas. He knows himself. When he proclaims that the plight of World Jewry is *really* unsettling to him, he backs up the claim with his holy insomnia.

Many of us toss and turn at night because of problems we face that seem unsolvable, doubts we experience that appear unfathomable, or fears we encounter that just won't go away. It is very disturbing. But we seem to lose sleep as a result of tension, rather than concern. What a shame.

Ironically, losing sleep can be one of life's greatest wake-up calls. It should cause us to reflect on some of the really pertinent and personal questions we often avoid.

"What matters most to me?"

"Why do I worry and what can I do about it?"

"Can I relinquish control over things that are truly out of my hands?"

"Does my daily routine accurately reflect the priorities in my life?"

"If I truly believe in the Creator, why does my behavior in so many arenas not attest to that conviction?"

Rosh Hashanah, it would seem to me, is a time to not only face the A-mighty, but a time to face ourselves. This year, don't count sheep or sip wine — use the time to ponder...and maybe even answer the questions that really count.

And if you're having trouble with that, you can always look heavenward for help. After all, you're horizontal anyway...might as well open your eyes.

To Tell the Truth...
Sort Of

I'm confused.

People say things and I tend to believe them. People do things and I don't question their intentions. Is there anything wrong with that? Does that make me naïve? Optimistic? Gullible? Trusting? I had to find out.

And so it was, not long ago, that I set out one Sunday morning, list in hand, ready to "ACCOMPLISH."

Crossing Coney Island Avenue, on my way to several stops, a bold looking sign in a store window caught my eye.

"SALE! QUILTED COMFORTERS $14.99!! TODAY ONLY!!!"

Comforters were not on my list, but having an extra one is always a good idea, I thought. Especially since it was cheap and was on sale for just one day. But as I stood outside the store contemplating this major purchase, I realized that I was pretty sure that I saw the same sign in the same window yesterday...and, come to think of it, two days ago as well. I guess the sale was extended. I walked on.

The sun was baking the sidewalks of New York and I ducked into a convenience store for a quick drink. 11:00 a.m. was a bit early for my Diet Pepsi, so I opted for something a bit lighter. The words *"Contains REAL Juice!,"* printed in banana yellow, grabbed my attention. I bought two. It was only about 10 minutes later, when I sipped the final dreary droplets, that I noticed the other side of the label — *"2 percent juice"* it read. Oh well.

I hadn't bought a lottery ticket in quite a few years, but this was hard to resist. It would really be nice to win $132 million, I reasoned. And for a measly $1 investment — well, the math made sense. The clerk passed me a pencil and I scientifically selected my winning entries. Just prior to making my final decision to enter, I read the bottom line of the card. I assumed it was an optional request, perhaps even comical.

> *Please select your preferred method of collection. Check one:*
> ❑ *1. One lump sum*
> ❑ *2. 20 annual payments*

But when I handed in my Mega-Millions ticket, the man behind the busy counter wouldn't process it. *"C'mon,"* he snarled. *"Can't ya read? How do ya want your money? All at once or over 20 years?"*

"Do I really have to decide now?" I asked. *"Can't we wait until the drawing, JUST IN CASE I don't win?"* A feisty senior citizen with vivid and bushy eyebrows appeared beside me and muttered, *"Manipulation — that's what it is, you know. They ask you how you want the money now, to get you thinkin' that you really have a chance of winning. Subtle...very subtle."*

I just smiled and filled in "one lump sum." Hey! You never know!

Just then, my cell phone rang. It was Aaron. He was in the car, on his way to a conference in White Plains. He asked how I was feeling, but I'm not sure he heard my answer. The reception wasn't that great. We shmoozed about nothing, as I waited for the purpose of his call. It never came. But I thought it would look cheap if I asked what he wanted, just because I had a small number of minutes on my plan and he had unlimited.

"I'll let you go," he offered after about 25 minutes, as I heard the car door slam in the background. I suppose he reached his destination. It was nice hearing from Aaron.

I took care of half a dozen little chores in the next two hours and by then it was time for that Diet Pepsi. The line was long and the mercury was soaring. Finally it was my turn. *"Jumbo it,"* I instructed the fountain attendant as I wiped my sweat with a frayed napkin. He filled me to the top and thanked me for the exact change in one swift motion and off I went with my 24 oz. cup. Curiously, 20 seconds later, by the time the foam settled, the cup looked nearly half empty. *"Be optimistic,"* I thought. My cup was literally half full — not half empty. Besides, the kid was probably in a rush.

By late afternoon I arrived home, turned on the radio, and sat down to sift through a pile of recent, yet still unopened mail. And it's a good a thing I did. Many of the envelopes said, *"IMPORTANT!"* and *"DATED MATERIAL ENCLOSED!"* and *"SPECIAL OFFER!"* Naturally, I opened those first and read them extra carefully.

One letter suggested that I could actually save a whopping 83 percent on a "U.S. News" magazine subscription. I wondered why I merited being selected to receive this most extraordinary offer. And why the publisher would be willing to practically GIVE his magazine away. He's got to be losing money by offering an 83 per-cent discount! The small print revealed the answers. The reduc-tion was based on a comparison with those customers who would purchase "U.S. News" every week for three years for full price at a newsstand. I guess there must be someone out there who does that. Don't you think?

Another correspondence, this one from Delta Airlines, stated quite clearly that I could fly to any destination in the world and take a companion along ABSOLUTELY FREE! Now that's what I call an incredible deal. The fact that this offer was being made only if I bought a full fare ticket was, admittedly, somewhat disappointing — especially when you consider that one full fare ticket typically costs quite a bit more than two of the usually available discounted fares. Oh well — my wife doesn't really like traveling anyway.

When I put down the pile of envelopes, I was better able to focus on the news that was blaring in the background on the radio.

"Coming up — a special report on a shocking medical break-through that will change the way we live," said the animated anchorwoman.

It was then that I realized that she had said the very same pro-motion three times in the last 15 minutes...without ever getting to the special report. I wondered to myself why I was so impatient. If she said that the report is "coming up," then that's exactly what it means. She never said WHEN the report is coming. So why did I have a problem with that?

A commercial for Orajel followed.

"Why wait 30 minutes for Tylenol to take effect," asked the announcer, *"when Orajel can begin soothing your baby's teething pain in just 5 minutes?"*

Now there's a reasonable argument if I ever heard one, I thought. That is, until I asked Raoul, my local pharmacist, if their claim was true.

"Oh sure," he said. *"Orajel works faster. But Tylenol's relief probably lasts about 10 times longer."*

Hmm. I wonder why the announcer failed to mention that. Maybe he just didn't know. After all, most announcers are not pharmacists or pediatricians.

The day was winding down when my doorbell rang. It was my neighbor, Harry. He was just stopping by to invite me and the family to a barbecue at his house on Wednesday evening. Most of the neighbors were coming too. It was nice of him to include us. And if not for my niece's wedding we would have loved to go. I thought I had told Harry about the wedding a couple of weeks ago. I guess he forgot.

Lying in bed that night, I thought back to the events of the day. *"Why are people always so skeptical and suspicious?"* I thought. The Torah teaches us to be precise and meticulous in every word we say, in every way we do business and treat each other. Shouldn't the secular world also share that very same value system? That drink did, indeed, have real juice in it. And yes — Aaron was just schmoozing me — not using me. And there's no way that soda clerk can wait for everybody's foam to settle. And some people DO buy "U.S. News" at the stand. (And those same people probably pay full fare when they travel.) And I could easily have missed that report on the shocking medical breakthrough, just like Harry forgot about the wedding.

"Naïve," you say? No way. I just refuse to let these things affect me.

I was heading off to bed, and my wife wished me good night.

"You're wonderful!" she said.

I wonder what she meant by that.

Did You See Darya in the Stairwell?

"G-d, hold our heroes in the palm of Your hand."
(Scribbled on the backdrop of the Ground Zero V.I.P. Viewing Stand)

*T*his is *not* a story about September 11th.

It was *supposed* to be, but it just didn't turn out that way. Allow me to explain.

My desire...need...urge...wish...to visit Ground Zero was born early — late September, I think. Like many others, I knew I just *had* to go there, but I wasn't sure why. Access to the concrete graveyard was, of course, severely restricted at that time, but maybe that was part of the peculiar allure that gripped me over three months ago.

"I'll go soon," I reassured myself.

October came. Succos, weddings, deadlines, daily nightmares in Israel, kids' homework, seminars, war, conferences...October went.

Friends went. They reported back to me.

"The rubble itself must be ten stories high."

"I couldn't see much, but it didn't matter. The vile smell was enough."

"We all just stared in silence. There must have been hundreds of us."

I heard their descriptions. They were punctuated by pain, enveloped in emotion, and searing with uncertainty. But somehow...they just didn't sink in.

"In memory of those who gave the ultimate sacrifice."
(Scribbled on the backdrop of the Ground Zero V.I.P. Viewing Stand)

November arrived. Time to begin the "research." How do you get there? When's the very best time to go? Who should I go with? Where did I put my old shoes? Do I have any "connections" that can get me *up close*?

Where does one park? What is my REAL PURPOSE in going? Is it wrong to take a camera? Binoculars? Are my children ready for this? Can the new Mayor Bloomberg ever fill Rudy's shoes?

The fine line between *research* and *rumination* was fading fast. So was November.

In therapy, they call it *resistance*. You *think* you want to change, but the fear is too great. Could I be *resisting* the very urge I wanted so much to satisfy? Could I be avoiding the startling visual and visceral stimuli that could ultimately be utilized to help generate genuine life changes? Impossible. Seeing the carnage that can penetrate the deepest recesses of the soul is not only something important; it's something I really *want* to do! I just want to go when it's "right."

"Did you see Darya in the stairwell?"
(Scribbled on the backdrop of the Ground Zero V.I.P. Viewing Stand, next to Darya's picture)

Along comes December. The Taliban is tumbling. Anthrax is slipping to page 23. Global warming meets New York City. The Dow rebounds. And the 24-hour Ground Zero work teams forge ahead. The buried pockets of endless smoke are no more. Wood planks of various sizes are shaped into official spectator viewing sites. The final standing charred remnants of the North Tower are dismantled and reunited with their crushed beams and mortar. Ten stories of rubble are dumpstered, dissected, and carted away. The crew is already months ahead of schedule.

Predictably, I intensify my plans for the inevitable visit.

The day arrives. The calendar reads January 4, 2002. It is 115 days after that unforgettable Tuesday morning — about 80 days later than I should have gone. The sun is brilliant...again. I find my old shoes, but I no longer need them. Even with the police escort that I was able to arrange, I get no closer than the V.I.P. Viewing Stand. I felt like I was in Row W of the bleachers at Wrigley Field. But on this day, there were no players on the field. The game, you see, was long over.

Oh sure. There was plenty of work going on. Cranes in place, trucks shuttling back and forth, a security guy fumbling with a stubborn, wind-blown American flag, etc. And images of the specter of what took place nearly four months ago did dance through my mind as I leaned over the makeshift railing. But the game was clearly over. No striking evidence, no real remnants of the horror, no smoke…no tears. I felt embarrassed. I looked down at the dumb, old shoes I had donned for the occasion and just shook my head.

> **"Steven, I miss you so.**
> **Please help me to be strong for our Emily."**
> (Scribbled on the backdrop of the Ground Zero V.I.P. Viewing Stand)

I stood there for about 30 minutes. I had reserved two hours for the visit and hoped it would be sufficient. My 25-year-old son, Naftali, stood beside me and feigned emotion. Neither of us spoke. But our thoughts were the same: *"We missed the boat."*

I thought back to the beautiful lesson attributed to the Baal Shem Tov, 18th-century sage and founder of the Chassidic movement. Small children are the paragons of purity on this world, he said. We grow up and forget what it is like to be a child, unencumbered by conflict, shame, and pride. But observing the daily activity of any healthy child can afford us some wonderful reminders of what life should be like. Three important lessons emerge:

First, when you *really* want something, cry for it. Kids are relentless in their demands.

Second, approach every situation with vitality and freshness. Their *get-up-and-go* attitude prevents boredom from seeping in.

Third, kids want everything NOW. Their inability to put things off for later can be frustrating to parents, but it is often a blessing in disguise and a powerful message to us. Never…ever…delay.

Lesson number 3 haunted me as I took one final gaze at my lost opportunity. I so much wanted to see something that I could take home with me. A vision…a memory that would impact me forever — perhaps a tidbit of morbidity that could remind me to treasure every precious moment of life. But it was too late for that.

I pulled my scarf a little tighter around my neck. A slight wind blew and the temperature was a couple of degrees above normal. But it felt a lot colder than it really was and I knew it was time to leave. I turned to Naftali. *"I'm glad we came,"* he lied. We both grinned a little and he shrugged his shoulders. My old shoes led me back to the steps. I looked at the scrawling on the backdrop as I left, desperately seeking some parting message of inspiration or consolation. The handwriting was painfully young.

"Dear Daddy, I miss you. I love you."

This was supposed to be a story about September 11th. I was hoping to learn something from the visit.
    Strangely, I think I did.

"This Is Where I Buy My Coleslaw"

A Formula for Change as an Aid to Getting Married

rue. Nobody said it was going to be easy. But then again, nobody warned you about how long and painful the trip would actually be, either.

But how could they have known? After all, each journey is so unpredictable; there really is no way to properly prepare for it.

The voyage, of course, is *shidduchim* (getting married) and the seas have never been more turbulent than they are now. The plight of ever-increasing numbers of older singles in our midst has now become a full-grown scourge. And the agony is rampant.

"Ki ayn bayis asher ayn shom..." Practically no home exists that is not, in some way, affected by this growing epidemic — if not directly within the nuclear family, then certainly indirectly, through extended family, friends, or neighbors. Not surprising then, that well-meaning people everywhere ask, "Why? How did the situation become so grave? Can't we figure out what happened? Why are *many thousands* of serious, capable, and mature young men and women in the Torah community finding it so difficult to find their life partner?"

And yet, the etiology of this crisis seems, to this writer, to be rather moot. The causes are probably so diverse, so complex, and so beyond consensus that it appears fruitless to expend endless energy to *solve* the mystery of the unmarried. Instead, let's focus on solutions. *Why* they find themselves in this dreadful predicament is far less important than relieving their pain and helping them build their own *binyan adei ad* (everlasting home). If my son has a fever, I don't ask why. I give him some Motrin, pump him with fluids and send him to bed. *Later*, I conduct the investigation.

With that in mind, let's talk about the most frightening six-letter word in the English language. It is "***change.***" Do you feel the pain? Are you frightened? **C-H-A-N-G-E.** It's terrifying. It's alarming. Most of us physically cringe when we hear the word. Panic sets in.

> *"Change? **I** should change? Why should I change? What did I do wrong? Maybe the change will be **worse**? What am I supposed to do? Can't I just try again? Give me one more chance. I'll try harder this time. I'll do **anything**, as long as I can keep doing it the same way."*

You and I, we humans, are creatures of habit. We like uniformity. We like consistency. We like familiarity. We even like repetition. We like knowing what to expect from the world. We like knowing what to expect from each other, and what to expect from ourselves. It makes us feel safe and secure...in a world of diminishing safety and security.

Truthfully, all of us practice this habitual behavior in ways that are both subtle and apparent.

> *"This is where I buy my fish. This is **my** fish store."*
> *"Why not try going to...?"*
> *"Oh, no. Why would I want to do that? I always go here."*

And in case you're not much of a fish lover, try on one or more of these ever-so-common habitual and ritualistic declarations.

> *"This is when I wake up...every single day."*
> *"This is how I drive. That's just the way I do it."*
> *"This is where I daven. I wouldn't go anywhere else. This is how I daven. I daven the same way...every single day."*
> *"This is where I buy my coleslaw. Why would you go anywhere else? I like this coleslaw. That's just how I like it."*
> *"This is when I go to sleep."*
> *"These are the zemiros that I sing...**every single week**. The same zemiros."*

"This is the thought that I say at the Shabbos table about this parashah every single year. Over and over and over again."

"This is how much tzedakah (charity) I give. That's how much I give. It doesn't matter what the appeal is for. That's how much tzedakah I give." (Which is fine if you're giving $50,000 to every appeal, by the way.)

"You know what? This is me. I like me. I like the way I've been doing it, so I'm going to keep on doing it. Every day, every week, every year... erev, vavoker, v'tzaharayim (evening, morning, and afternoon)."

And that's how we go through life.

And you know what? There's really nothing wrong with it. It's called consistency. It's beautiful. *I'm a consistent person.* They call it *kvius*, in Hebrew.

"Es hakeves ha'echad taaseh baboker, v'es hakeves hasheni taaseh bein haarbayim..." (a reference to the two daily offerings brought in the Temple) every single day. And that's how we are.

But like most things in this world, there is a downside to this life-gestalt, a side effect. Our *Chazal* (Sages) warned us about it. Our *neviim* (prophets) warned us about it. They called it *mitzvas anashim melumadah* (performing mitzvos with oblivious regularity). The dangers of *hergel*, doing things by rote — without thought or contemplation. Almost robotic. Regular. From the word *regel*, or *hergel*. "Be careful," they said. "Don't do that."

"But if it's working," you're saying, "what's wrong with it?"

And you're right.

But that's exactly the problem. Let's say it's *not* working. What do you do *then*? Let's say you're *not* married. Let's say your children are not married. Let's say they're not *close* to getting married — and they want to, so much. Or let's say they're *always* close to getting married...both are equally difficult.

Let's say you're not even being *redd shidduchim* (no potential matches are suggested). And we know people like that. Or they are always being *redd* the wrong ones, who don't share the same goals, the same values. What then? What do we do then? Isn't there a time, as difficult as it is, when we have to look at ourselves, and look at our children, or look at our grandchildren, and say, "You know what? This is not working." There's something wrong.

Let's be clear. We're not talking about *blame* here. No fingers are being pointed and no hypotheses of fault or responsibility are even being suggested. Nobody really knows.

But there is a time when you have to be honest with yourself. You have to say something is wrong, something is not working. That is very hard to do. Why? C-H-A-N-G-E. Admitting that something is really not working implies that something needs to be changed. Perhaps only for the sake of change, but change, to be sure. And that is upsetting.

An example from the Torah — from the prototype of all *shidduchim* — Eliezer in his search for Rivkah.

Eliezer has concluded his pursuit. He witnessed enough miracles and attributes of *chessed* (kindness) to make him certain he has found "THE ONE." There could be no doubt that only Heavenly intervention brought him to Rivkah. But as the agreement is about to be consummated, Eliezer utters an astonishing charge to Lavan and Besuel, Rivkah's brother and father, respectively.

"V'atah im yeshchem osim chessed v'emes es adoni, hagidu li..." If you think this is a good idea, and you're ready to do *chessed v'emes* with my master, tell me about it.

"V'im lo, hagidu li..." and if not, tell me.

"V'efneh al yamin o al s'mol," and I will veer to the right or to the left.

Amazing. He sees all the Heavenly signs. He has *kefitzas haderech* (miraculous shortcuts). He sees *nissim* (open miracles); the waters are rising from the well! He sees Rivkah performing countless acts of distinguished *chesed*.

"Hashem hitzliach darki," declares *Eliezer.*

Hashem has made my mission a success. There's no question in his mind. This is it. And what does he say? "Tell me if it's good. Because if it's not, we'll move on. *V'efneh al yamin o al s'mol.*" Rashi says, "We'll go to *bnos Lot* or *bnos Yishmael* — Lot's daughters or Yishmael's daughters."

Rav Avraham Pam adapts the particulars of the story. Eliezer could not have been more certain that Rivkah was the right match for Yitzchak. The *Hashgachah* (Divine intervention) could not have been more clear. And yet he was fully prepared to search elsewhere, should it not work out, for some reason. The flexibility was extraordinary!

How often, says Rav Pam, have we been witness to a situation when a *shidduch* is as close to completion as is possible…when suddenly it breaks up, *Rachmana litzlan* (G-d have mercy). Everyone involved is crushed, and understandably so. Depression often sets in and blame is quickly assigned to an assortment of persons, sometimes only remotely involved in the process.

But while the situation feels and certainly seems tragic, we cannot lose hope or the ability to transcend the pain.

"V'efneh al yamin o al s'mol." Eliezer had every single sign you could imagine. And what does he say? Sometimes you have to change. We'll go to *bnos Lot.* We'll go to *bnos Yishmael.* If that's what we have to do, that's what we'll do. We'll move on — a lesson of immense proportions.

Admitting that we are truly stuck is enormously difficult, but the key word here is flexibility. We've got to be ready — *V'efneh al yamin o al s'mol."* And not necessarily with a major metamorphosis — just with enough change to give the *Hashgachah Pratis* a new opportunity in which to work.

The changes relevant to these circumstances fall into two basic categories: attitude and action. While no one can lay claim to a declaration that any single attitude or action is *wrong* or even *inappropriate*, it can be said with certainty that adhering to any attitude without knowing *why* it is that way is unhealthy and counterproductive. A person's mind-sets need to undergo periodic scrutiny and investigation to ensure their validity and relevance.

Attitudinal examples that demand examination and analysis can include any of the following:

> *"I want only a tall boy."*
> *"I need a rich girl."*
> *"I don't like blondes. It's just not me."*
> *"I cannot marry someone with a beard. It's impossible. I just can't do it."*

And we convince ourselves that it's impossible, simply because we've *always* thought that way. It is the syndrome of, *"This is where I buy my coleslaw."* I know a lot of people who got married without a beard, but things do change!

"I will never marry a boy with an up-hat...or a down-hat."

Never say never.

"I will only go out with a 'professional.'"

While similar intellectual pursuits can often add luster and compatibility to a marriage, this factor is far from being definitive. How many people do we know who are employed in businesses, but also happen to be great teachers, at home or with their peers? And how many social workers or nurses are there who are stymied by apprehension, yet constantly dream about entrepreneurship? Let's remember how terribly unscientific relationships really are.

"I could never marry a baal teshuvah."

Again, this is another ill-advised *philosophy* or *myth*, that the differing backgrounds of those who have been *frum* all their lives and those who have *"joined the fold"* spell marital disaster. Nothing could be more untrue. Often times it is precisely the combination of the two divergent experiences that nourishes and nurtures the relationship. A true fulfillment of *ezer k'negdo* (contrasting partner).

"What? You're 'redding' me this girl? Wasn't she once engaged?"

Yes, she was. What does that mean? Is she not allowed to make a mistake? Even a major mistake, if it was one? Of course there are times when a broken engagement may be a signal that a certain problem (probably not insurmountable) may exist, but it does not and should not imply a patent disqualification. Previously engaged men and women deserve a chance.

Those who have *never* been married often have a particular resistance to marrying those who *have* been married, especially if they have children. Divesting yourself of *all* candidates in that category is yet another illustration of the *"coleslaw* condition." Had Boaz felt the same way about Rus (Ruth), the lineage of David HaMelech (King David) and even Mashiach would have been inexorably altered. Something to think about.

A true change in attitude means focusing on the *person,* not on the *baggage.*

Changing our *actions* in pursuing a mate can, at times, be relatively minor. Maybe it's a simple thing. Maybe it's a tie, a dress, a hairstyle or a different location for a date. Maybe your dates should be shorter. Maybe your dates should be longer. There are people who are day people and people who are night people. Perhaps you should consider dating more in the daytime, instead of at night.

Maybe *what* you do on the date should be different. Maybe you should be a little more open on your dates; or a little *less* open on your dates. Maybe you need to ask more questions or perhaps you are too busy trying to impress, instead of finding out more about the person you are considering. Or maybe you need to go to the organization called *Invei HaGefen*, the sensitive and wonderful address for serious, older singles — uncomfortable, though it may be.

It is true. Dating is not coleslaw. And changing time-honored patterns in attitude and action to improve one's marriage potential is far more daunting than changing the *zemiros* we sing. But questioning our habitual behavior, even in a small way, can open the door to the more significant alterations that we need to make.

Of course, sometimes your actions need to be a little more dramatic. Today networking is the engine that moves the *shidduch* process along. And, difficult as it is, a change of venue may be indicated. New people. New *shadchanim*. New opportunities. New mazel. Moving cannot be ruled out.

Some older singles have a desire for greater introspection. Are there subconscious, underlying causes that may be creating a barrier to getting married? Or are there specific thought-patterns or behaviors that need to be understood or modified? Therapy, with a licensed, qualified, and Torah-true psychotherapist can help, often through a short-term modality. Conversely, singles who have been in therapy for a while may need to consider a change in therapists or even terminating treatment, if stagnation has set in.

A final consideration involves a serious review of your dating history. All too often, a name of someone you met years ago is dismissed as "not for me." But people do change. Your needs may be different now. His priorities could have shifted. The passage of time, life experiences, and a solid dose of reality, can accelerate the maturation process. Taking a careful look at each name on that list can be surprisingly prudent. Many stories exist where two people, having met 10 or 15 years earlier, have subsequently married. You could be the protagonist of one of those stories.

Nobody is very comfortable with change. Those old house slippers, threadbare and holey though they may be, still feel kind of snug and cozy. But if you're serious about adding another pair of slippers to your closet, and a devoted partner to your life, those torn relics may need to be discarded. In their stead just might be a shiny new pair of dancing shoes.

Learn Torah –
Win a Lexus SUV!

*A*round the world, but especially in the U.S., there has been in recent years a virtual explosion of programs available to help us learn more about our Jewish heritage, traditions, and significance. A plethora of tapes, books, seminars, retreats, websites, and CD's, trumpeting the beauty of our religion are easily attainable in nearly every region where a Jew resides. It is truly remarkable.

But the staid, formal lecture-series of yesteryear seems to be going the way of the land-line phone and the double-breasted suit. Increasingly rare is the educational event that does not feature (or at least advertise) a celebrity appearance, pregame sushi, enhanced audio/visual effects, or Kabbalah. Some organizations have even coined the term *edutainment* to describe their method of curriculum development!

What's going on?

I suppose we should not be surprised. Such is the way of the world. If you want people to come, you've got to give them what they want. And what do they want? They want excitement, allure, the exotic, some action, perhaps even the peculiar.

O.K., so we're not surprised. But the question I have is, *"Why?"* Why must we dress up something that really should sell itself? Shouldn't the absolute wonder and truth of Torah be sufficient to attract the masses of meaning-seeking souls among us? And furthermore, this phenomenon of needing charming enticement and beguiling persuasion is not limited to attendance at educational functions. We even do it to ourselves at home. And it is equally perplexing.

As much as we might enjoy the time we spend listening to an informative tape or CD, or reading a really fascinating book, essay, or Torah concept, or logging on to a spectacular Judaica website — somehow, we often resist doing it again. It defies any rational explanation.

It usually goes something like this.

> *"So, let's see…last night I spent 45 minutes listening to a fascinating tape about the Torah's view on euthanasia. It made me think about things I had never in my life considered! Like the value of time, the human potential, what a 'soul' is, and stuff like that. Truthfully, it was the best 'therapeutic hour' I had experienced off the couch in a long while.*
>
> *"Hey! Here's a CD of a talk given by the very same speaker! He was great. This one is about how the Patriarchs dealt with sibling rivalry. Sounds rather appealing; something I am sure to enjoy.*
>
> *"Well…on the other hand…those weeds in the backyard sure do need my attention — they look so neglected, the poor things. And isn't tonight the night our neighbor is showing their wedding video for the fourth time? I wouldn't want to miss that!"*

You get the picture. No matter how much we truly enjoyed delving into a Torah concept last night, tonight everything else… ANYTHING else, appears to be more enticing. ABSURD, but oh so true. And that's why the PR guys are "forced" to fancy up nearly every program that tries to teach us something really important and help us understand life better.

It reminds me of a talk once given by Rabbi Noach Weinberg, dean of Yeshivah Aish HaTorah in Jerusalem.

> *"What is your greatest pleasure in this world?" he asked a group of parents.*
>
> *"Our children, of course," they dutifully answered in unison.*

"And what is your greatest pain?" he inquired further.
"Why, our children, of course!"

He was making the point that contrary to common belief, pain and pleasure are not opposites. They are actually very closely connected. More often than not, we cannot access genuine pleasure without expending the effort. So he pushed the audience just a bit more. Choosing a newly married couple, Rabbi Weinberg asked them a very personal question.

"Tell me, if you don't mind, how many children do you think you'd like to have?"

They thought for a moment, whispered a bit, and then cooperated.

"Three, maybe four," was their honest response.

The audience applauded.

"That is truly beautiful," remarked the rabbi. *"But tell me,"* he pushed on, *"if having children is so gratifying, why wouldn't you want 14 or 15 of them?"*

He paused...then continued, not waiting for their response. *"What's wrong? Too much pleasure...or too much pain?"*

The answer was, of course, quite obvious. Most of the time, when faced with a pleasurable experience that requires real effort, we end up surrendering to our disdain for pain. In other words, too often we are really not pleasure seekers; we are just *comfort* seekers.

For most of us, learning Torah — be it on a tape, from a text, at a lecture or a class, or from a website — pleasurable though it may be, still rings our internal *work* bells. As a matter of fact, studying *anything* probably stirs within us some negative associations related to our school days — where demands, expectations, exams, homework, competition, *REPORT CARDS (ugh!),* marks, and parental disapproval were the order of the day.

So, to a certain extent, we all suffer from PTSD (post-traumatic stress disorder, scholastic type) that just won't allow us to fully *enjoy* a valuable learning experience. That's why those Mozambique llamas suddenly seem so fascinating.

We need to remind ourselves that those days are over. The deprogramming must begin. You will not be graded when the class is finished (I promise). Your parents (or children) will not be apprised of your progress or your deficiencies. You can even leave the class early WITHOUT A NOTE FROM HOME!

The insights and wisdom awaiting you are incalculable. Torah is not some esoteric or cryptic course of study. It is not designed to make you feel oppressed or guilty or even sophisticated. It is neither a lesson in history nor a voyage in mystery. It might astound you; at times it will confound you. But more than anything else, studying Torah is like making a new and great friend.

And like a great friend, Torah is not only dependable, consistent, and fascinating, it really speaks to you. There is no topic, no matter how contemporary, innovative, or complex, that it does not address. It is the ultimate instruction manual, written by the Manufacturer, disseminated by His most trusted Think Tank, and cherished by His loyal constituents for more than three millennia without pause or interruption.

So next time you get the urge, the tug, or the notion to open a page or two, don't expect your brain to simply give you the *"full steam ahead"* message. It just doesn't work that way. A venture this profitable will bring some conflict with it. That's O.K. Consider yourself reprogrammed and ready for battle. It is a war well worth fighting.

Let the games begin. Victory awaits you.

Confessions of a Reject

I hope you don't mind if I am perfectly honest with you.
Good. Here goes.

I am a reject.

There. I said it. And now you know.

As a practicing psychotherapist, I am committed to an oath of *patient confidentiality.* After more than 20 years in practice, I've got more secrets stashed away in my psyche than your local rabbi and the Israeli Mossad put together. So I guess I've grown accustomed to keeping things (especially embarrassing things) pretty much to myself.

But no more. In a spirit of spontaneous candor, I've decided to waive my own rights to confidentiality (perfectly legal) and reveal to you the story of my most recent rejection.

Curiously, it happened, of all places, at **Aish.com**. But only a handful of people know about it. That is...until now.

I've been writing for Aish.com for a while now and frankly, it's been a nice ride, as they say. Some good responses, interesting feedback, creative outlet, maybe even some personal growth (not to mention the inadequate pay, to boot). Sailing along, I guess.

A couple of weeks ago, I read an article about robots in the *U.S. News & World Report.* And I thought, "Why not write an article about the special qualities of the human condition and why robots, no matter how sophisticated, could never really be a substitute for man and his *neshamah* (soul)?" A little different. Bordering on "trendy, with a dash of depth," perhaps. I wrote it. I liked it. I submitted it.

Brace yourself for the next turn of events. You guessed it. "REJECTED!!!"

It seems the vote was unanimous. No one on the "Editorial Committee" liked it. Not a single person. "Not different...not trendy...no depth."

Now rejection is not a feeling that I am overly familiar with. Oh, I *deal* with it all the time. Rejection in *others*, that is, but not myself. And for those of you who are equally new to this sensation, allow me to inform you that it is not a particularly pleasant experience.

> *"People **are** interested in robots."*
> *"What do **they** know about depth, anyway?"*
> *"They're not just rejecting my article. They are rejecting **ME!**"*

Overreaction? Perhaps. But short-lived, thankfully. Recovery was rather swift. But emerging from the dust of the episode was some serious contemplation about the immense power contained within this most potent emotion.

Every segment of our lives is really a breeding ground for potential rejection. Our marriage, our children, our jobs, our friends, our teachers, classmates, peers, store clerks, bank tellers, bus drivers, etc. Whosoever we interact with is really a prospective rejecter. Yes, it's a jungle out there. Rejection could occur at any time.

And the response by the one rejected runs the gamut from impervious Teflon (as in, *no stick*) to mortal injury. Everyone is hurt when he is excluded from a group, his ideas are laughed at, or a serious relationship is terminated. But not everyone feels discarded when he "fails" jury selection, watches his soda getting stuck in the vending machine, or is served second by the waiter. Hypersensitive responses to those and other similar situations are better termed *paranoia* than *offended*.

But let's face it; no one is going to be invited to *every* function in town. We will all tell jokes that *some* people will find entirely unfunny. And who hasn't raved about a speech or a tape or a book that *somebody* has found to be totally inane or just plain boring?

Upshot?

Rejection is here to stay. We had better find ways to deal with it.

Here's just one way. Focus on the positive.

One of the elements that is slowly vanishing from the American scene is sincerity. Everyone seems to be seeking sincerity, but it is not easily found.

> *"Do you like the way I did my hair today?"*
>
> *"Sure! It's terrific! It's really...er...uh...really...eh...**YOU!**"*

Or how about...

> *"I'll pick you up at 6. We can go to this new Kosher Tunisian Health Bar on the south side. It's really different. All they serve is carob dishes, 56 different varieties of carob. Can you imagine? What do you think?"*
>
> *"Sounds very special! I'm really in the mood for carob tonight."*

Of course there's nothing wrong with being polite and accommodating. Some of my best friends are polite and accommodating (not too many, though). But a more *sincere* response, while still not impolite, might have been, *"Sounds very special! But I'm **not** much in the mood for carob tonight."*

Yes. That reply *might* make your friend feel rejected, but you'll score big sincerity points when you tell him next week that you absolutely loved the steak house you went to.

Sure. It's a trivial example. Sincerity is only faintly significant when talking about hairstyles and eateries. But the same lesson applies everywhere. Surviving the injury when the group doesn't laugh at our "favorite" joke only serves to sweeten our pleasure when they howl in hilarity the next time we tell our *new* "favorite" story. *"They really liked <u>this</u> one,"* we may conclude.

How many of you have shared a *really special* Torah thought, at the Shabbos table or just in passing, and have received, in return, blank faces, gestures of bewilderment, or a totally unexpected vitriolic counterblast (all in good cheer, of course) that totally confounds you? Again, your capacity to rebound with resilience will open the passage to fully appreciate when your next attempt is met with nods of approval and words of praise.

In other words, the occasional and inevitable rejections in life help remind us how good it feels to be genuinely accepted, wanted and loved.

The Torah goes so far in expressing the importance of open and honest communication that rebuking our friends when they do something wrong is actually one of the 248 positive *commandments*! We're often not even permitted to ignore a wrongdoing we have witnessed. And which commandment do you think is written immediately after this one? *Love thy neighbor as thyself.* G-d wants us to understand that being critical, in a truly constructive way, is not mean or inconsiderate. It is an obligation! One that is an extension of the love we must feel for each other.

I must admit. Receiving the news that **Aish.com** could do fine without my robot piece, thank you, did not create overwhelming feelings of gratitude on my part. But it did remind me that acceptance is not automatic. When they like something, they really do like it. That feels good.

Meanwhile, if you would like to read a great piece about robots, just write to me in response to this article (ysalomon@aish.com) and tell me why you are interested. I'll email the article to the three contestants with the best answers. The rest of you will just have to be rejected. Good luck!

"You're on the Air!"

*I*f my picture appeared on CNN tomorrow and was broadcast instantly to hundreds of millions of viewers worldwide, I wonder how many people would recognize me.

Well...let's see. There's my wife, my mother, my in-laws, my brother and my kids (and their spouses), and my dentist (if I'm smiling in the picture). That makes 17. Add in some friends, some patients, a few friendly neighbors and certain blood cousins and other relatives and the total might reach three figures — not a whole lot of people.

Of course, not everyone is as unrecognizable as me. I remember reading a while back that the words most easily understood in the world were *Coca-Cola*. And the face most easily identified was that of heavyweight champion Mohammad Ali. (I hope Ronald Reagan didn't feel too bad.)

I haven't seen any recent polls on the topic, but my guess is that the person most universally recognized today is probably Osama bin Laden. The recognition of this mastermind of evil is instant and globally wide-reaching.

One of the most fascinating dynamics of the entire bin Laden saga is what has happened post-9/11 and a lesson that he might be indirectly teaching us.

More than 3½ years have already passed since that unforgettably horrific morning in Lower Manhattan, the Pentagon, and Shanksville, Pennsylvania. To many, me included, it seems like just yesterday. The sun shone brilliantly that late summer day in shocking disparity to the devastation that would soon be wrought upon the Western world. It took only minutes for hundreds of millions of people to realize that life as we knew it would never again be the same. It wasn't.

The catastrophe and eternal upheaval for the thousands of grieving families is, of course, immeasurable, but the consequences for the rest of the world have been far-reaching, as well. In a very real sense, every one of us has become a virtual hostage to this fiend. It feels as if we will never really sense total safety again. And although most of us no longer leap to our feet and gasp when a loud noise invades our moments of reverie, we are still very much on guard, on edge, and *on the lookout.*

Truthfully, it baffles the mind. Why should it be this way? No one is totally comfortable in saying it, but with the exception of a few rather feeble and isolated anthrax scares, these shores have been eerily safe and absent of terrorist activity since that dreadful September morning of 2001. Alerts come and go, color codes become elevated and diminished, pronouncements and cautionary directives are issued and are usually ignored, elderly ladies are randomly searched by airport screeners, and cabinet departments are assembled and dismantled, but through it all, all appears to be quiet on the Western front...thank G-d.

But there is one small blip on the panic screen — the periodic audio and visual tapes, allegedly recorded by OBL, and released by Al-Jazeera. It seems that he just won't go away. Every so often another tape is mysteriously born and disseminated, and that's when the "fun" begins.

Regular programming is interrupted when the "news" breaks that "HE" has spoken. Linguists, speech-pattern experts, and intelligence pundits are immediately summoned to lend testimony to the relative veracity of the said tapes.

> *"It is bin Laden's superb and special Arabic language that is very hard to emulate," says one authority typically. "It is undoubtedly his voice, his style, and the standard examples from history that he uses."*

More and more spokespeople are often paraded in front of us to offer their sage opinions about the true identity of the voice (or the picture).

And once the consensus is reached that it is indeed OBL who has addressed us, then the *main course* is served, as the analysis of the "message" ensues. Each and every word is systematically sifted, lifted, picked apart and torn asunder. The nuances, pronunciations, and even the facial expressions of this diabolic puppeteer are discussed, interpreted and reinterpreted.

"Is he really still alive?"

"Did he seem angry?"

"What did he mean when he urged Muslims to 'liberate the Islamic world from the military occupation of the Crusaders'?"

And so it goes. The color code shifts to red, worldwide security precautions are reset, and some universal breath-holding is dusted off and reinstated for a while.

When you stop and think about the whole episode, it is nothing short of incredible. This warped power monger literally holds the entire civilized world on a short and frayed string. All he needs to do is wake up in the morning and sneeze and the Neilson ratings become totally reorganized. His every utterance is noted and decoded; his every move is feared and focused on. Imagine if he said something that was *REALLY* important.

We can observe this phenomenon and marvel at his power. We can take note of this trend and laugh at the absurdity of it all. But what we really should do is *learn* something from it. After all, isn't that the real reason it is happening?

Nearly all of us (a safe, polite way of saying *all of us*), have had the experience of going to a doctor to check out something that we were worried about — a nagging cough, a persistent headache, a funny skin discoloration, hair loss, etc. More often than not, the doctor examines, asks some stock questions, shrugs and tells you to forget about it.

"It should go away in somewhere between 14 days and 2 weeks," is his usual not so funny and hardly reassuring prognosis. "If not, call me and we'll run some tests."

But no matter what his exact words are, most of us leave the office and immediately begin our anxious ruminations — picking apart everything the doctor said like he had recited the Gospel.

"What does 'should' go away really mean?!"
"Why did he have to qualify it by saying, 'if not'?"
"What kind of 'tests' was he talking about?"

The point being that some people, like doctors, and even more so like Osama bin Laden, are in a position where every single word they say is so incredibly weighty that people's life plans are directly and supremely linked and affected by them! This is not unlike the innocent reflections from Federal Reserve Chairman Alan Greenspan — whose off-the-cuff, cavalier comments about the bond market or the yen can easily fling world economy into a sudden upswing or a devastating tailspin.

Just pretend, for a moment, that you had that kind of power. Imagine if you were so important (or so feared) that the whole world stopped to hear whatever you were saying. How careful you would be with your choice of words, your tone of voice, your inflection and even eye movements, if you knew that those around you would be watching, listening, recording you, and analyzing you like a hawk.

Well, guess what? They probably are. It might be your spouse or your kids or your roommate or your colleague, but there are people close to you who are undoubtedly deeply affected by the things you say and the words you use. You may not realize it. You may not believe that people take you that seriously. You may *prefer* to deny your impact on others, but that is the reality.

The applications of this notion are as diverse as the words you use to communicate with. You may pay little mind to how you react to your husband's solution for Sammy's lack of friends, but maybe you should. Dismissing it as "ridiculous," or "impractical," or "another one of your *brilliant* ideas" may be far more hurtful and callous than you realized or intended. And children, even at a very young age, are keenly attuned to how you respond to *everything* they say — no matter how silly or inconsequential it may seem.

The Talmud (*Sanhedrin* 37a) teaches us that we are all directed to say and believe, "The entire world was created just for me." This is not meant to encourage arrogance and conceit. Rather, it is an enjoinder to help us realize our enormous responsibility to everyone we encounter and to the Jewish People as a whole. To many people — more than you think — you really are their whole world.

And Pesach seems like the ideal time of year to dedicate, or re-dedicate ourselves to this aspiration. Everything about the Seder seems designed to help us focus on our speech — telling the story of our Exodus, describing the miracles, asking questions, featuring the children who must listen AND ask their own questions, etc. Even the protagonist of our story, Moshe himself, was uneasy about his ability to speak effectively to Pharaoh because he stuttered!

Indeed, the word Pesach is actually a compound word composed of *peh sach,* which means a *mouth that speaks.* And, of course, the entire evening is centered around a book that walks us through this magical night — called the *Haggadah* — the Hebrew word for *telling.*

You may never appear on CNN. And you might never be a worshiped sports hero or a fugitive mass murderer. But make no mistake. Your words count. People are listening. Their emotional well-being, their mood and temperament, and even their feelings of self-worth can sometimes hinge on what you say and how you say it.

It is a responsibility of mammoth proportion.

Don't fear it. Embrace it.

Succos in Spanish Harlem

*P*eople who know me know that I grew up in an apartment building in Manhattan, on 105th Street between Columbus and Amsterdam Avenues.

I enjoy telling people that because of the reaction it usually elicits.

"Spanish Harlem? You grew up in Spanish Harlem?"

"Man, that's a rough neighborhood. Did you get beat up often?"

"Nah, you must mean West End Avenue and Riverside Drive, right?"

I sort of wear my roots like a badge of courage or a medal of martyrdom, shocking people with the notion of a scrawny, Brillo-haired, yarmulke-clad kid living in the "jungle" with inner city delinquents and rabid Jew-haters. Those familiar with the neighborhood, then and now, typically conjure up visions of daily, if not hourly altercations with ex- or soon-to-be convicts, leaving the poor "Jew-boy" lying bloodied on the pavement, barely breathing.

Not quite. I do enjoy the shock value and accompanying commiseration/admiration that invariably follows, but my childhood memories are totally devoid of these dramatic battles. Quite the contrary, I walked to yeshivah every day, skipping to the thumping bass sounds of Tito Puente blaring from the fire-escape transistor radios. I bought my Drake's Devil Dogs and Fanta Orange soda from Felipe at the bodega next door. And I spent after-school hours in front of my building playing stoop ball, skelley, and stickball with my best friend Osvaldo Garcia and the rest of the gang. I was not exactly *roughing it.*

Oh, occasionally I'd hear a disparaging epithet hurled from a passing Pontiac, but by and large life was peaceful for the Jews on the Upper West Side in the early 60's. We did our homework, loved the Kennedy's, knew the cop on the beat by his first name, and basically minded our own business.

Among the other fond memories I treasure is the annual Succos experience we enjoyed. We were just a handful of observant Jews among the 60 families, mostly Cuban, in 120 West 105th Street, but we relished the opportunity to build and decorate the *succah* which was neatly nestled in a corner of the concrete yard that framed the rear of the six-story structure.

As best as I can remember, Uncle Leo was in charge.

To this 9-year-old, Uncle Leo seemed like a Jewish combination of Bruno Sammartino and Killer Kowalski. And when he schlepped the dozen or so solid pine panels for the *succah* walls (he wouldn't let anyone help him), I marveled at his strength. It was a good couple of years later that I discovered that Uncle Leo was probably only a domino or two taller than 5'6", but to me he was a giant. Adding to his machismo no doubt was the imposing black holster that draped his left shoulder, exposed when he lifted the weighty wood. (He worked as a diamond dealer.) Somehow the bulky revolver within it didn't frighten me. I'm not sure why.

Of course, the rest of the *succah* crew pitched in as well. Some helped with the construction, led by Juan, the Puerto Rican superintendent; others brought the tables and chairs. The placement of the *schach* (covering) — consisting of many heavy leafy branches from Central Park (in the pre-bamboo era) — required the muscle of several able-bodied youngsters. I just pretended to help and protested a bit too much about being overworked. And let's not forget about the decorations committee who never got enough credit for beautifying this "temporary home" of ours in a décor of simplicity and refinement, on a shoestring budget. I guess life was just innocent and uncomplicated.

Meanwhile, in fourth grade, just a few blocks away, I dutifully (sic) studied Torah, social studies, etc, and learned about the laws and meaning of Succos.

> *"It is true that we build succahs to commemorate how the Jewish People lived in the desert after the Exodus from Egypt," instructed Rabbi Newmark. "But Succos is much more than that."*

My little ears perked up a bit.

> *"The whole point of moving into a shaky hut, with a rickety roof, is to remind us that our safety and security don't really come from bricks and concrete — four walls and a firm roof — they really come from Hashem."*

I wasn't quite sure what *security* meant, but I think I got the point...somewhat.

That year was just like every other. The *succah* stood tall, the leafy branches were in place and the decorations hung neatly. Succos was here once again and the unassuming immigrants of 105th Street, most of them Holocaust survivors, proudly led their small families into the frail, but holy, shelter. My excitement was boundless. Outside, the enormous moon seemed almost happy that the Festival of Joy had finally arrived.

Inside, an air of formality prevailed. It always started out that way. Even though we were all either relatives or good neighbors, there was something about eating all together and displaying our simple utensils, wardrobes and foodstuffs in public that created a fragment of apprehension. But that faded quickly.

The scene was comfortably familiar. Mommy opened the plaid thermal bag with the not-so-hot chicken soup and wondered aloud where the heat went. Daddy sang the usual melodies — some upbeat, some maudlin. Cousin Willy assumed his customary rank as Captain Mischief. And my brother and I kind of sat quietly, soaking up the scene.

I don't remember exactly when it happened. I just know it was swift, sudden, and unforgettable.

The meal was nearing its end. The conversation was ordinary and the spirited strains of selected holiday tunes were fading into the cool night. The white tablecloths, once glimmering, were now sullied with assorted remains of horseradish, grape juice, challah crusts, and half sour pickle ends. The happy moon was shining softly through the breaks in the flimsy roof branches.

And then it hit. Out of nowhere, a boulder, flying faster than a comet, came hurtling through the *succah* roof! Beams cracked. Splinters flew. Glass from plates and bulbs exploded in the air. Darkness fell over us. And the horrified shrieks of panic frightened me. The crash had shattered everything in sight — especially the serenity we loved so. Miraculously, no one was hurt.

The shock was incredible. Some cried, some breathed heavily, some held their heads and eyes. The fifteen or so of us all kind of froze in place. The only one I remember moving was Uncle Leo. Like a blur, he rumbled past me out the *succah* door, like a man on a mission.

Trembling from fear, I held onto Mommy. The entire incident had lasted just a second or two, but I knew the impact would be felt forever. I stared at the broken folding table and fixed my tear-filled eyes on the huge rock that lay beside it. It was bigger than a football and probably weighed 20-30 pounds. Had it hit someone, G-d forbid (like me), it could have killed him. It was a scene I shall never forget.

It was some time later, perhaps days, that I thought back to what Rabbi Newmark had taught us:

> *"The whole point of moving into a shaky hut, with a rickety roof, is to remind us that our safety and security don't really come from bricks and concrete — four walls and a firm roof — they really come from Hashem."*

It was a concept that we 9-year-olds had difficulty understanding — especially when everyday life seemed so serene and tranquil. But that night in the *succah* I learned a painful lesson. Having friendly neighbors, police officers, and friends is a wonderful thing. Living in a big, strong, apartment complex can make you feel safe. But *true* security comes only from Hashem.

It is a concept that *all* of us need to remember. We go through life believing that a concrete roof, a 401K, a car alarm, a security fence, or a PhD. will be our eternal guarantee for safety and success. And those may all be valuable strategies to pursue. But we forget, or *prefer* to forget, that we are not really the *true* determinants of our ultimate destiny. We get lulled into complacency, like me when I was 9 years old.

It is a tender memory that still haunts me, but every year now, when I build my own *succah*, I am at peace. I know that whatever I do, I am but a small star in a much larger constellation. It is the A-mighty Who dictates our destiny.

I sit in my *succah* and still catch a glimpse of the big, friendly moon above. I smile and teach my children — the youngest is 10 — that sometimes we will understand His ways; other times we will be bewildered. But Succos is about surrendering our delusions of grandeur and placing our trust in Him.

Somehow, that feels good.

Building Your Own Temple

*L*et's be fair.

To fully appreciate this article, you really have to know Chanala...and not just because she's my daughter. But suffice it to say that whatever she does, she does with passion and enthusiasm and animation...and plenty of it.

And so it was that a few months ago, when her sixth-grade teacher, Miss Fried, detailed the assignment to the class, Chanala was leaping out of her seat like a sizzling slice of pizza on an unsuspecting tongue.

> *"The Tabernacle we are learning about, which the Jewish People built in the desert," explained Miss Fried, "was just like the two Temples that would stand in Jerusalem many generations later."*

Chanala and her classmates were getting their very first exposure to the concept of the Temple, which served as the focal point of Jewish life, practice, and service for a total of 830 years until the year 70 C.E. First impressions can last a lifetime and Miss Fried was especially adept at making every important lesson come alive for her girls. So depicting the Temple as something more than just an ornate physical structure or even a big synagogue was a challenge she rather relished.

"Could you imagine if we — this class of sixth-grade girls — would actually build the Temple? Wouldn't that be unbelievable?"

Not everyone fully understood what Miss Fried had meant. They knew they were not builders, engineers, architects, or contractors, so how could they be expected to build the Temple? "Besides," whispered one girl, "I heard that only Mashiach will be able to build the Third Temple!"

"Allow me to explain. I'm going to divide the class into small work groups. Each group will meet at night and build a small model of a section of the Temple. Then, in two weeks, when the parts are completed, we'll join together. Each group will bring and present her project to the whole school. We'll join the parts and create a magnificent model of the entire Temple!"

By this time the entire class was buzzing with anticipation and delight. Miss Fried announced the participants in each group and what section they would be asked to complete. Chanala and her three friends were assigned to construct the *Mizbach HaNechoshes*, the Copper Altar, with its monumental and majestic ramp. (I thought it not coincidental for Chanala, since the Altar just happened to be the main hub of activity in the entire Temple — rather fitting.)

Chanala could hardly wait to come home from school and tell us all about the thrilling project. In fact, she didn't — she called from the school pay phone during recess. She described every minute detail of her new sacred mission (as she is wont to do), and asked if the group could meet in our house (of course) TONIGHT, to begin working on the model. How could we say no?

A few hours later the front door burst open and four female, boisterous, budding sixth-grade construction workers came barreling into the living room, tripping over each other's words and bodies. What a sight it was.

"I'll get some scissors."
"Where is the oak tag?"
"Look! I found a great color diagram of the Temple in this book!"
"Can we stay for supper and sleep over tonight, tomorrow, and the next day?"

Truthfully, it was all rather adorable. The zest with which these girls embarked upon their new venture was vivid testimony to their teacher's enthusiasm and to their own zeal for learning.

The team toiled for several hours that first night of work, with not a lot to show for it. To their credit, they labored on their own. The toppling configuration looked like a cross between a crippled piano and an early creation of the Wright Brothers, but never did any of them even consider asking for assistance or for our opinion. Good for them. This was their baby and they were going to keep it that way.

Undeterred, the quartet finally parted for the evening, determined to get a better handle on the situation on the following night. To state the obvious, falling asleep, for Chanala at least, was no simple task — too much buzz, anticipation, and adrenalin. The rest of the group, we heard, had similar experiences.

Progress was slow but consistent over the next few nights, as the girls' creativity started kicking in. By the end of week one, the model actually approached a level that could almost be called 'recognizable." And as a bonus, the group also began studying the purpose, splendor and meaning behind the Temple service as it related to the Altar and its diverse offerings.

But the clock was ticking away. With just a few days left to complete their venture, the girls worked at a feverish pace. Our dining-room floor had been literally transformed into a full-time manufacturing plant/assembly line, with varying amounts of Styrofoam, matchsticks, double-sided tape, cellophane, DucoCement, tape measures, and wood shavings strewn all over the place.

Their own crude diagrams served as blueprints for the holy endeavor, and judging from the crescendo of voices that animated the final hours of production, these 11-year-old draftswomen were learning incredible lessons that were as much about collaboration and deference as design and assembly. It was something to see and to admire.

As week two drew to a close, the Altar, ramp, and all of their compartments and trimmings were nearing completion. Everything had been measured, cut, formed and bonded. The detail was actually rather impressive. I'm not sure if a museum curator would have paid big money for it, but for a group of idealistic sixth-grade neophytes, they had a lot to be proud of.

It was the night before the deadline and the smiles on their little faces told a delightful story about determination, achievement, and pride. Chanala could hardly get the words out:

"We are ready to paint!"

Armed with cans of spray paint and shielded by aprons of holiness, our heroines triumphantly marched outside, assuredly transporting their creation through our front door. My wife and I watched from the kitchen with recriminations for not having videoed the occasion for posterity. They had really done it — and all by themselves.

It was almost suppertime and the autumn shadows had nearly completed their transformation to darkness. We knew that the whole painting process would not take long and soon the troop would be calling us outside for our very first look at the totally finished product.

But when the call came…it was hardly the one we expected. The shrieks shook us to our bones.

"MOMMY!!! TATTY!!! OH! NO!"

We flew out of the house and found four howling girls flooded with tears.

"Look!" shouted Chanala, pointing down the block.

We crooked our heads to the right and saw the model, already in many pieces, bouncing down the street — ensnared in a gust of wind. Some sections were lodged under parked cars, others were stuck in bushes. Some pieces apparently were already gone forever.

"It came out of nowhere," screamed the hysterical girls.

"One minute we were spraying the paint — the next minute it was gone."

"I tried running after it, but the wind was just too fast for me."

I scooted down the block to retrieve the irretrievable, but it was to no avail. Moments later I returned with the shattered remains of a valiant project that was somehow just not meant to be. Needless to say, the girls were inconsolable.

The cleanup was a sad one. We salvaged some of the vestiges of value, more for reminiscence than utility, and after several minutes we trudged back into the silent house. There really was not much to say. The helplessness kind of said it all.

Over the next few hours the girls were all picked up. They returned home empty-handed. Chanala skipped supper and went to bed. Outside, the wind was calm.

My heart broke for her as I sat beside her and stroked back the forlorn curls that had cluttered her tear-stained cheeks. Her feelings of loss were profound and I treated them like those of any full-fledged mourner.

We processed the events of the last two weeks and remembered all the glorious and gleeful details of the undertaking. Together we recalled what the structure looked like in its first few days and she actually laughed at the thought. Healing had begun. It was obvious that the pain would remain for a while, but I also knew that recovery would follow soon after.

I kissed her good-night and told her how proud I was and how much I loved her. I could see her smiling in the glimmer of the night-light. Walking out the door, I thought of one more thing I could say to her. I stopped and considered the implications. "Was it too early? Is this something that she can hear now? Was I overdoing it?" I wasn't sure, but I decided to tell her.

I turned around and headed back to her bed. I sat down once more.

> *"You know Chanala, tonight was a very sad night for your friends and for you. Right now, all of you are in a lot of pain. And when you are hurting, Mommy and I are hurting too. Someday, when you'll be a Mommy, you'll understand that even better.*
>
> *"But, as much as you are all hurting now, could you imagine, for a moment, what all the Jewish People felt, 2000 years ago, when the REAL Temple was destroyed? You built a model of an Altar in two weeks — they lost everything. The Temple was their home for over 400 years!"*

I didn't have to wait long for the reaction. Her face was a strange mixture of wonderment and anguish. She looked up at me and covered her mouth. I thought I heard a gasp. She understood.

I kissed her again and left the room. I didn't suggest to her that maybe, just maybe, G-d had chosen the model's destruction as a vehicle to teach her and her friends and her parents and her class and countless others the impact of the events of Tishah B'Av and the destruction of the First and Second Temples. How could I know if that was true?

But I have a feeling that those little girls, on that windy night, in their overwhelming sorrow, came a lot closer than most of us ever will, to really understanding the true meaning of Tishah B'Av.

Go for the Gold

*P*eople often wonder why G-d no longer speaks to us directly.

Ha.

The year is drawing to a close and Rosh Hashanah, once again, is nearly upon us. I would think that G-d would find a way to communicate with His children. I'm sure he has a message or two for us. All we have to do is listen in.

And so I did...listen, that is, as did hundreds of millions of others worldwide, who also followed the Summer Olympics. Not that I would call myself an ardent badminton or kayaking fan. Truth be known, I cannot locate Slovenia on a Rand-McNally nor have I ever lectured on the relative skills related to quadruple sculls repechage rowing vs. women's 25M pistol shooting. But rather than appearing un-American, I just followed along.

Looking back, the date was August 18, nothing remarkable about that. But it also happened to correspond to the first day of the Hebrew month of Elul — exactly 29 days before Rosh Hashanah. Coincidence, I guess.

The scene was the Olympic Indoor Hall in Athens. Never in history had the United States ever taken the gold medal in the coveted Men's Artistic All-Around Gymnastics competition. Twenty years previous, Peter Vidmar had won the silver, and now the spotlight centered on an unassuming, freckled-faced gymnast from Waukesha, Wisconsin, named Paul Hamm. An imposing field of twenty-three aspiring competitors hailing from South Korea, Kazakhstan, Israel, and Cuba — to name just a few — came to the Games with equal grit and fortitude, and, undoubtedly thousands of hours of arduous training, with eyes on the very same goal.

Adding to Hamm's pressure were the shocking early disappointments that the heavily favored Americans had already suffered in men's and women's tennis, men's basketball, and several swim meets. The good 'ole U.S.A. could ill afford yet another unexpected defeat and Paul Hamm knew it.

The Artistic All-Around consists of six separate rotations, each, of course, watchfully judged and scored, after which the final tallies determine the medalists. Hamm did not disappoint. He came out like a beacon at midnight, scoring a hefty 9.725 (out of 10) on the opening Floor Exercise, good enough to tie for 1st place at the outset. His momentary skid to 2nd place after the Pommel Horse hardly concerned him as he vaulted back into the lead after the Rings competition.

Three events were now completed and three were left. The stadium scoreboard showed Hamm's name on top and the faces of the others in varying shades of fatalistic pessimism. No one believed that they could actually wrestle the lead away.

Hamm readied himself for rotation number 4 — the Vault. He had no inkling that unimaginable disaster was just seconds away. Leaping backwards, Hamm executed perfectly 1½ somersaults in the air. The elusive "Gold" was inching closer. Then, like a razor-sharp blade diving into hot butter, he segued effortlessly into his landing phase — something called a Tsukahara, with two and a half twists, extremely difficult — with a blind landing. Shockingly, Hamm hit the mat crouching and never could establish balance. His legs tangled and he stumbled to his right, heading ironically and directly into the judges' table, where one of the judges was forced to use his own hand to fend him off. It was like taking a road test, driving perfectly, and finishing by crashing into the examiner's car...only a thousand times worse.

A glazed look of horror washed over his face. The score of 9.137 undoubtedly finished him. The crowd gasped as Hamm plunged into 12th place. The dream was over.

How often, in life, do we dream of accomplishing something really important, yet fall short of our expectations? How many times do we imagine *winning the gold*, only to find ourselves tangled and stumbling into the judges' table? How many Rosh Hashanahs have come and gone with our list of "New Year's Resolutions" looking exactly the same as the previous year's list?

Too many, I suspect. And what is our response to our perennial failures? More often than not, the human condition kicks in with the usual letdown and predictable disillusionment.

"What's the point?" we wonder. *"Change is just too difficult,"* we declare. *"Greatness is for really great people — not for me."*

What a pity. How different the outcome could be if only we felt inspired...inspired to keep dreaming and determined to firmly believe that there exists no obstacle before us that cannot be overcome.

Apparently, Paul Hamm had the dream and the determination.

He sat teary-eyed and dejected, his proud, hunched shoulders grazing the arena wall. Years of hoping, and waiting with bated breath, had washed away in an instant. Two final events remained while eleven champions-to-be smugly blazed the path ahead of him. Perhaps there was ample time to, at least, regain some composure and self-respect, but certainly nothing more than that.

But somehow, Hamm shook off his crippling despair.

"I just went for it," he explained later.

Boy, did he ever. How he managed to flirt with perfection on the Parallel Bars, arising from the depths of defeat, defies explanation. His score of 9.837 was the highest in the event and catapulted him from twelfth to fourth place overall. The remarkable comeback was suddenly within reach. It seems Hamm had saved his best for last.

Grasping the High Bar as if his life depended on it, he attacked this final routine as never before. With the crowd on its feet sensing history, Hamm executed flawlessly, completing three straight blind release moves that startled even his own coaches. He spun off the bar, landing on the mat as if it were a giant suction cup. The masses roared. The matrix board flashed a 9.837. Hamm held his head is total disbelief. The miracle was his. GOLD!

The Jewish calendar is, in great measure, a lunar one. Indeed, the Jewish People, in its storied history is frequently likened to the moon. It is said that just as the moon is "reborn" after a period of decline and apparent disappearance, so too Israel's tragic decline will also end, and its light will blaze to fullness.

In fact, Israel's ancient history bears a startling resemblance to the moon. There were fifteen generations from Abraham to King Solomon — at which time Israel rose to unprecedented greatness (like the full moon at fifteen days). Immediately after, their decline began until it reached its depth in sadness fifteen generations later with the destruction of the First Temple (completing the cycle).

The moon's lesson of disappearance and rebirth is one we must carry with us forever. Perhaps that is why Rosh Hashanah, the pinnacle of our spiritual revival process, is designated to occur on the first day of the month. Never can we allow despair to engulf us — not individually and not as a People. That is the hallmark of ushering in a New Year.

Curious. This unprecedented Olympian comeback *just happened* to occur on the first day of the lunar month of Elul, the very beginning of the sacred period for introspection and repentance.

I believe that G-d very much *wants* us to remember that giving up is simply not an option. And He has, in His holy arsenal, an infinite amount of avenues, vehicles, and messengers (maybe even one paradoxically named, "*Ham*[*m*]"), that He can employ to help deliver this most poignant communication.

Watching Paul Hamm in his moment of international humiliation should give us pause. Watching Paul Hamm, minutes later, in his moment of boundless glory, should give us hope. Somewhere in between, he met the judges face to face.

People often wonder why G-d no longer speaks to us directly. Ha.

Passover: Homeland Security for the Jewish People

J have a friend. Let's call him Mark. Mark was actually my first friend in this world. We met in kindergarten…46 years ago.

Mark was special and everybody knew it. Tall, bright, studious, witty, athletic, and well-mannered without being nerdy, which was a big deal then, since this was the 50's and pretty much everyone was nerdy. If kindergarten would have had yearbooks, Mark would have been selected many times over in the "most likely to…" categories.

And so it was. Excelling in just about everything, Mark eventually chose law and climbed his way to the top in seemingly effortless fashion. No one blinked when, soon after graduation, Mark landed a top position as a litigator in a world-class Manhattan law firm. He had married, had children and was now making "a few bucks."

All seemed well…until one Passover. Mark was sitting at the Seder with his immediate family, some less-immediate relatives, and several guests. And not unlike many a Seder experience, the *afikoman* tradition was again a hallmark of the evening's majesty and spiritual glory. Adhering to the time-honored custom, Mark's children "stole" the broken piece of matzah FROM RIGHT UNDER

THEIR FATHER'S NOSE and then refused to return it unless he granted them their most special wish. The preparation, the act of larceny itself, and the ensuing, most-contrived investigation kept the children involved, energized, and most importantly, awake for the long night's service and unforgettable grandeur.

A hush descended upon the shimmering dining room as Alex, age 7, approached his father for the revered annual *afikoman* negotiations.

"What would he ask for this year?" everyone wondered. "A two-wheeler? A first baseman's mitt? Perhaps dinner at a semi-fancy eatery?"

It was anyone's guess. All eyes were fixed upon the angelic youngster. You could see his exuberance dripping from every expressive feature he possessed. Mark steadied his long arm around Alex's tiny waist and looked lovingly into his soft eyes.

"Tell me, my son, what is your wish."

Alex returned his father's gaze and swallowed twice. The old grandfather clock ticked louder than ever before. Alex blinked a few times and then spoke. His voice quivered ever so gently.

"I have two wishes," he announced with increasing resolve. "First of all, I want Mashiach to come."

The guests laughed quietly. Mark smiled.

"I share your wish, Alex. I really do. Now tell me your second request."

Alex looked down and swallowed again. He seemed awkward and tense...almost afraid. His voice dropped, but he got he words out.

"I wish so much that your office would burn down."

No one spoke. The collective gasp was inaudible, yet shattering. Eyes darted to every possible distraction in the room. A cousin cleared his throat. Someone poured an unnecessary glass of grape juice. And Mark slowly slipped his arm from Alex's waist as shiny tear balloons crowded Alex's huge eyes.

Mark excused himself and retreated to the den. He understood the request. He understood very well. It had been four years since he first took the position. The hours were long...very long, at first. 7:30 a.m. to 11 p.m. was not an unusual occurrence. But that would stop, he knew. They *told* him so! And his wife — she understood too. It was the price they had to pay. But the long days never ended. Perhaps they never would. And meanwhile, the years were slipping away. And Alex just couldn't stand it anymore.

Most of us fathers do not work 15-16 hours a day, although many mothers do. And few of us have an expressive child like Alex to shock us into sanity. But the kids around us — be they our own, our nephews and nieces, or those in our neighborhoods — have had a pretty tough year. Threats from al-Qaida ring in their fearful little minds. Snipers appear in their dreams. Gas masks replace lunch boxes. Unemployed fathers snap at the slightest provocation. Green, yellow, orange, and red are no longer playful colors — they are frightening *codes*.

- Who will comfort them?
- When will we soothe their increasingly fragile psyches?
- How will they rebound from near-constant terror and develop to their full and secure potential?

In response to the collective concerns of American citizens, the United States Congress, this year, created an entirely new division within the Federal government known as the *Department of Homeland Security*. Hundreds of millions of dollars have been allocated to help Tom Ridge and his staff ensure our safety and security. But our fears, somehow, remain. And our children still feel exposed and in danger.

The Jewish People are no strangers to this frightening phenomenon. Indeed, it has been part and parcel of every day of our fragile existence for thousands of years. Even the *Haggadah*, read at the Seder when we celebrate our most dramatic emancipation, reminds us that *"In each and every generation there are those who hover over us to annihilate us."*

But the sentence that follows reminds us of the comforting reality. *"The A-mighty continues to save us from their hands."*

Perhaps Passover can be dedicated as the occasion to make our kids feel safer. After all, this is the holiday that highlights the significance of transmitting to our children every miraculous detail of our flight to freedom. This is the festival that underscores the generational bonds that have kept our People vibrant and our traditions meaningful. The entire Seder, in fact, is predicated on a process of questions and answers, of storytelling, of capturing the interest of the children so that they will inquire, understand, and some day, relate the story themselves.

Maybe Passover, then, can become the *Homeland Security* for the Jewish People, especially the children, with the Seder its main arena.

No matter how long, elaborate, or spiritual your Seder is — it is certainly a rare and special opportunity. How often during these most hectic times do we get a chance to gather peacefully, with family and friends, for several hours, and celebrate life? Why not use the opportunity to rededicate ourselves to our future — our children?

> *Give them attention — undivided.*
> *Give them love — unconditional.*
> *Give them time — unrestrained.*
> *And give them hope — unending.*

They need it now more than ever. And Passover is the perfect time to do it.

By the way, a few weeks after that impassioned plea, Mark gave notice at the firm. He entered the nonprofit sector and today uses his talents to benefit the worldwide Jewish community. He's a leader and a role model for thousands of admirers. His office did not burn down. It was just refurnished.

Alex is now a bona-fide Torah scholar, happily married with children of his own. His second prayer was answered. Now we all hope for the first.

The Magnificent Sevens of Shavuos

*I*n the beginning...G-d created sevens.

Oh sure, He created the light and the heavens and earth too, but for reasons unknown to us, He seemed to have a special affinity for the number 7, and for groupings that seem to center around this numeral.

The fact that He began His Torah with a verse containing seven words...28 letters (divisible by 7) is hardly remarkable, but when placed within the context of the overwhelming number of associations in Judaism with "7," a fascinating tapestry begins to unfurl. Let's take a closer look at this phenomenon.

⌘ WHY "SHAVUOS"?

This week, Jews around the world celebrate the holiday of Shavuos, commemorating the most seminal event in the history of mankind, God's Revelation at Mount Sinai. It became the crowning moment, as the Jewish People became a Nation.

Shavuos. Curious name for this holiday, no? Shavuos means weeks, underscoring the seven-week period between Passover and Shavuos in which we count each day (and week) in anticipation of and preparation for reliving the Revelation. But why call it "Shavuos/Weeks"? Call the holiday "Torah"...or "Sinai"...or "Commandments"...or "Tablets," but **Weeks**? Of what significance is that?

Time contains many different entities. Nearly all of them are related to natural phenomena. Days, nights, months, seasons, years are all directly determined, in some way, by the constellations. There is one exception — the week. The formulation of a week seems to be totally arbitrary. Who needs it? Let one day just follow the previous one. And why 7 days?

The concept of a week constituting 7 days is one that is strictly G-d-invented and man-adopted. We may quibble about Creation — how, when, why; sadly, even by whom — but the world at large has consensually agreed to the concept of a week. And whenever a week is completed it is yet another reminder to mankind (or should be) that G-d created the world in 7 days. Only 6 days were required to actually manufacture the physical structures, but the process was not complete until the spiritual realm — Shabbos — was added.

∞ WHY "7"?

The Kabbalah teaches us that 7 represents wholeness...completion. After 7 days the world was complete. There are six directions in our world: north, south, east, west, up and down. Add to that the place where you are and you have a total of 7 points of reference. Shavuos, marking the emergence of the Jewish People into a nation, by virtue of their receiving and accepting the Torah, is therefore also marking a completion. Perhaps that is one reason why the holiday is called Shavuos (Weeks). We want to remember this holiday as a way of denoting the completion of the process of Nationhood of the Jewish People.

In honor of our own completion of the 49-day period of preparation for this holiday, let's enumerate some of the allusions to the number "7" within Judaism. While there are more, we'll just present...say...49 of them. How many of these do you recognize? How many more can you add?

∞ THE MAGNIFICENT SEVENS!

1. *Shabbos is the 7th day.*

2. *There are 7 weeks in the counting of the Omer before Shavuos.*

3. *In Israel we have 7 days of Pesach and Succos.*

4. Every 7th year we observe the Shemittah laws — the land lies fallow.

5. After 7 cycles of Shemittah, we have a Jubilee year (Yovel).

6. When a close relative dies, we sit shivah — 7 days.

7. On Succos we shake the 7 components of the four species — 1 lulav, 1 esrog, 3 hadassim, and 2 aravos.

8. Yisro, the 1st true convert, had 7 daughters and 7 different names.

9. Moshe was born and died on the same day — the 7th day of Adar.

10. Our succahs are "visited" by 7 guests — Avraham, Yitzchak, Yaakov, Moshe, Aharon, Yosef and David.

11. The Menorah in the Temple had 7 branches.

12. Achashveirosh, King of Persia during the miracle of Purim, held a party for 7 days.

13. There are 7 holidays per year — Rosh Hashanah, Yom Kippur, Succos, Chanukah, Purim, Pesach, and Shavuos.

14. In addition to the 613 Commandments, the Sages added 7 more.

15. There are 7 Noachide Laws.

16. At every wedding, 7 blessings are recited.

17. Each Shabbos 7 people are called to the Torah reading (aliyos).

18. The 1st verse in the Torah contains 7 words (and 28 letters).

19. The Torah tells us that our Matriarch Leah had 7 children — six sons and one daughter.

20. There were 7 days of preparation (miluim) inaugurating the Tabernacle in the desert.

21. The bride circles the groom 7 times under the canopy (chuppah).

22. Men wind the tefillin straps on their arm 7 times.

23. Moshe was the 7th generation after Avraham.

24. Each plague in Egypt lasted 7 days.

25. In Pharaoh's dreams there were sets of 7 cows and 7 stalks of grain.

26. The contamination period (e.g. of corpses or leprosy) lasts 7 days.

27. God created 7 skies ("I'm in 7th heaven!").

28. On Shabbos and holidays we recite 7 blessings in the Amidah.

29. There are 7 special species of produce grown in Israel — wheat, barley, grapes, pomegranates, figs, olives, and dates.

30. God created 7 continents in the world.

31. The 7 weeks of the counting of the Omer correspond to the 7 "Sefiros," the 7 spiritual emanations — kindness, strength, beauty, triumph, splendor, foundation, and kingship.

32. Noah sent the dove out of the Ark for 7 days to inspect the weather conditions.

33. 7 nations were banished from Canaan — the Canaanites, the Hittites, the Hivvites, the Amorites, the Perizzites, the Jebusites, and the Girgashites.

34. The Kohen Gadol (High Priest) sprinkled the blood of the offerings in the Temple 7 times on Yom Kippur.

35. The New Year (Rosh Hashanah) begins with the 7th month — Tishrei.

36. The Jewish calendar — basically lunar — has a cycle of intercalation that contains 7 leap years during every 19-year period.

37. God created 7 musical notes in a scale.

38. Upon the death of 7 relatives — father, mother, never-married sister, brother, son, daughter, and wife — a Kohen (priest) is permitted to become ritually impure.

39. We dance 7 circles (hakafos) on Simchas Torah.

40. The minimum dimensions of a valid succah are 7 cubits by 7 cubits.

41. G-d created 7 seas in the world.

42. Joshua led the Jewish People around the walls of Jericho 7 times before the wall fell.

43. Yaakov worked for Lavan for 7 years (twice) in return for marrying his daughters.

44. The Temple had 7 gates of entry.

45. We recite 7 blessings every day before and after the Shema — 3 in the morning and 4 at night.

46. The Talmud enumerates 7 women prophetesses — Sarah, Miriam, Devorah, Channah, Avigail, Chuldah, and Esther.

47. A Jewish slave regains his freedom in the 7th year following his sale.

48. We conclude our Yom Kippur prayers by proclaiming, "Hashem is God!" 7 times.

49. After a marriage there are 7 days of feasting and blessing — celebrated by the recitation of 7 blessings (Sheva Berachos).

No one is certain *why* G-d chose the number "7" to signify completion. All we can do is speculate, observe and marvel. For now, that will have to do.

Happy Shavuos!

Let's Go to the Video

*O*n a typical fall Sunday, over 700,000 of your fellow law-abiding, peace-loving, American citizens leave their families, their couches, and their worries behind them to personally witness 15 clashes of the National Football League.

Just a day before, millions...yes, millions more spent most of their Saturday at over 300 different stadiums from Abilene to Zanesville, Ohio, watching college students play similar games. Many of them sat on narrow wooden slat seats, while insulated by several layers of thermal apparel, only subsequently to be stuck in 3-5 hours of postgame gridlock on their way home. And they paid hefty cash for the privilege.

Add to this the tens of millions who, every week, sit glued to their Home Theaters (remember when they were called TV sets?) for the better part of the entire weekend — no matter how beautiful the weather, no matter what else (or who else) is being ignored — fiercely rooting for and against people they have never met, hardly recognize, or even care for.

Now, what actually drives so many people to idolize, revere, worship, emulate, and adore sports heroes is a study for another season and another arena (or stadium). And let's not get into a whole discourse about the relative plusses of spectator sports. Suffice it to say that the phenomenon exists, and many millions thrive on it.

Basically, we have the Greeks to thank. Like so many of our modern-day entertainment vehicles, the concept of competitive and spectator athletics, later popularized by the Romans, began with the culture of Greece.

The forces on Earth are similar to the forces of Heaven. Just as G-d set parameters within which the forces of Heaven have power — some having dominion by day, others by night; some on land, others in the sea — so too did He establish parameters for the forces on Earth. Every nation and kingdom was given an area in which it would manifest its unique talent and might. To one He granted wealth, to another wisdom; one had strength, another beauty.

Yefes (Noah's son) had seven sons — the fourth of whom was Yavan (Greece). For 1700 years, Yavan's descendants played an insignificant role in the world, until the emergence of Alexander the Great, who brought Greece to the pinnacle of world power, replacing Persia. Conquering many nations and lands, Alexander transformed his capital into a center of wisdom, science, and physical prowess.

Most of us know the story. At first the Jews, while physically subservient to the Syrian-Greeks, rejected Greek culture. They remained steadfast in their beliefs, practices, and ideals. But the allure was too great. Eventually, many of them succumbed to the overwhelming temptations that so contradicted their national spiritual persona. Forming a sect called the Hellenists, these people built altars for Greek idols, and eschewed the Torah lifestyle for debauchery and entertainment.

While the majority of our People did not follow the ways of the Hellenists, the spiritual damage they wrought was huge. But King Antiochus, dissatisfied with the Hellenistic influence, lost patience with the tiny, stubborn nation, and sent his powerful armies to subjugate and slaughter the Jews. Some fled and hid, many surrendered and converted, and tens of thousands were murdered in the scourge.

Miraculously, the Jews fought back and triumphed. Led by a small band of pious and courageous Maccabees, they inexplicably defeated the mighty Greeks, rededicated the recently defiled Temple, and rekindled the fractured spiritualism of the masses. And for the last 2200 plus years, we celebrate Chanukah annually in commemoration of these extraordinary events.

The victory, astonishing as it was, was not complete. The contamination that had punctured the lofty standards of the Holy

Nation generated a devastating pollution that would taint the Jewish People for centuries to come.

And in many ways, today's worship of sports teams and athletes can be traced back to that era — when the fascination and glorification of physical beauty and brute strength pierced through our mantle of sanctity. Chanukah, it would seem, would therefore be a most auspicious time to try to recapture some of that lost holiness.

This year, after we light our candles and perhaps sing a Chanukah song or two, maybe we can turn back the clock a couple of thousand years or so. After dinner (any of the eight nights will do), go back to your Menorah. Grab a comfortable chair and 5 minutes of relative quiet in your home (for some, that will be quite a miracle right there). Focus your attention on those tiny, little flames and imagine those brave Maccabees, who understood so clearly that living spiritually was something for which it was worth risking one's life.

Now try picturing what *your* highlight film will look like one day.

Touchdown passes? Seven-figure mergers and acquisitions?

A hole-in-one? Perfectly manicured nails?

A half-court buzzer beater? That dream vacation to Monaco?

The softball trophy? The car that ALL your friends envied?

Your annual skiing jaunt? The top 100 restaurants you ate at?

Those may be highlights for most people. But Chanukah is the perfect opportunity to script your own highlight film and make sure that OTHER scenes and experiences are featured.

A family's get-together in a restaurant is lovely, but hopefully you left a respectable tip for the waiter. Earning lots of money can be enormously pleasurable, but did you remember to include charity in your newly expanded budget. Who wouldn't be proud of a hole-in-one? But did it lead you to arrogance or humility?

You get the point. As producer, writer, director, and main actor, you get to customize your very own highlight video.

Why not make it an award-winning film?

Blasting the Worm

*I*f you want to know how much RAM you need...don't ask me.

If you need information on which active-matrix display is best...look elsewhere.

Just mention "Advanced Configuration and Power Interface (ACPI) equivalent to the TCP/IP File Transfer Protocol or a hierarchical, distributed database that contains mappings of DNS domain names to various types of data, such as IP addresses," ...and you'll find me in a different zip code. Clueless would be an understatement.

As a matter of fact, until fairly recently I hardly knew an Apple from a nectarine, or a Task Manager from Joe Torre. No. Computer literacy was not my strong suit. Still isn't. Oh, I can type an article (in a variety of lovely fonts and sizes) and respond to email (occasionally even using the *cut and paste* feature). I'm getting there, I guess, but frankly, if real trouble strikes — I'm like a *sh'liach tzibbur* with laryngitis — fumbling and ineffective.

And so, to cut to the chase, two weeks ago real trouble struck. At first, it seemed relatively minor — one of those temporary glitches that every computer occasionally spews forth. But within a few days there was no denying it — I had been affected, infected, invaded, contaminated, polluted, violated, compromised, assaulted, attacked, raided, molested, battered, and TAKEN OVER by the now infamous MSBLAST virus.

I sat at my desk, numbly staring at hundreds of emails from total strangers — many from very small African countries.

"ME?" I wailed. *"Little old me? The me who rarely goes online? ME? The proud owner of a hard drive that is still 98.6 percent free after 2 years? The me who often loses all of his work while trying to adjust his margins??? HOW DID THIS HAPPEN? Don't you have to live in the jungle to catch malaria? Why would a scheming and potent virus bother with little old me? Isn't that stuff reserved for behemoth users like Pfizer, Lexus, and Congress?"*

In short order, I reached out to the "techies" in my life. I guess we all have them. Those are the friends and relatives for whom we never have enough time. But when WE need THEM...

Those are the associates who answer the phone, hear our voice, and immediately respond with, *"O.K. Yaakov, what did you do this time?"* We gulp. We chuckle uncomfortably. Sometimes we feign some feeble small talk before we mumble, *"Just a quick question, Izzy. It'll just take 30 seconds."*

Forty-five minutes later you're both floundering in a sea of cyber-disarray, not sure whether to declare wholesale surrender or courageously (or hopelessly) suggest, *"Let's start from the beginning, shall we?"*

And so, the advice began pouring in.

"Reset your drivers."
"Reconfigure your properties."
"Change your default settings."
"Delete...defer...and RE-BOOT!"
"Just go online and follow the simple 42-step recovery instructions!"
"PRAY!!!"

Truthfully? Everyone meant well. And some people actually seemed to know what they were talking about. But by the time the dust had settled — several days later — my monotonous New Times Roman resembled actual Roman Times and my trusty laptop Touch Pad was now more frozen than a lifeless chromosome of King Tut's mummy. Motility was impossible. I was completely stuck.

In the ensuing days, I learned that I had actually not been infected by a virus at all. Turns out, it was a "worm." What is the difference? Don't forget to whom you are talking — I have no idea. All I knew was that I needed a remedy.

To end your suspense, the story does have a happy ending. But, far more important, the ending tells a critical story.

Rosh Hashanah and Yom Kippur are just around the corner. These days of awe and reverence are marked by Jews worldwide with extended prayers, shofar blowing, and fasting. Most of us approach this segment of the calendar with feelings of dread and trepidation. And why not? If we truly believe that the A-mighty actually sits in judgment of us during these holiest of days and determines our every accomplishment or failure, what else could we feel but fright?

But maybe we need a little reframing of our Holy Days perspective. Maybe there's another way to approach our *Day in Court,* besides fear and apprehension. How about *Opportunity*?

Looking back on the past year, who among us hasn't slighted a friend, spouse, child, or neighbor? Who hasn't planned vast, or at least some minor changes in one's behavior...and failed miserably? Who hasn't forgotten, at various times, what it means to be grateful, ethical, faithful, or energetic? Indeed, who among us has not been infected by *a virus of the soul* or *a worm* that freezes our memory and internal hard drive?

G-d understands. He knows our limitations and our flaws. He recognizes our weaknesses and the trigger points that send us reeling backwards. And He says to us, *"Return."* Not only does He await and encourage our homecoming, he creates a process called *teshuvah* that actually gives us the chance to completely wipe the slate clean. With true regret, admission, and resolve we are able to start anew without *any* residue of past failing or transgression. A *tabula rasa* of the spirit. That is true mercy. *That is Opportunity!*

Eventually, the advice of the pundits worked. My computer recovered. The worm was exterminated, the virus arrested. Even my Touch Pad — the virtual legs of my computer — became mobile again. The secret? An incredible little function that the *Masters* over at Microsoft included in Windows XP.

Apparently, they understood that we mortals are quite fallible. They realized that the mistakes we make are sometimes so grave and so critical that patching them up would be fruitless and ineffectual. *"Why not give our patrons a method for them to just wipe their slates clean and start over?"* they reasoned.

And so they did.

They called it *System Restore*. A quick navigation through *Accessories* and *System Tools* brings you to this oasis of cyber havens. The startling and soothing instructions inform you that *System Restore allows you to undo harmful changes to your computer...and returns it to an earlier time without causing you to lose recent work, documents or email.*

No incantations, wands, or paranormal powers are needed. You simply peruse a calendar (included) and click on a date passed and *Presto!* All your settings are immediately returned to the way they used to be on that date.

True. *Teshuvah* does take a bit more than a pick and a click. But the mechanism for complete restoration of the soul is available to us. Viruses will always be trying to *worm* their way into our hardware. And new strains — more virulent and complex — challenge us to wage war and emerge triumphant. Perhaps that is the subliminal purpose of this far-reaching epidemic that has swept the world.

We may feel frozen, shut down, or bewildered by personal failures, dilemmas of mind or spirit, and dreadful world events. Terrorism rocks our symmetry of life. But G-d says, *"Never give up. Even when you feel paralyzed, there is hope. You will be up and running again. The virus, no matter how persistent, can be eliminated. The system CAN be restored."*

After all, *"teshuvah"* means *"return."* And we can all return to that place within ourselves when we knew we were on a higher level. It takes effort. It takes honesty. And you have to reach back a little and remember how really good it feels to be happy with yourself.

Just follow the directions, and add a good measure of prayer.

And then watch.

"Just Listen, Will Ya?"

*G*randpa was sitting alone in the kitchen.

It was a late day in May, but the mercury snickered at the calendar, like a leopard in a mousetrap. Everyone spoke about the heat, not really sure if it was a springtime anomaly or a harbinger of summer.

But Grandpa couldn't care less about weather patterning. He was, as we say, "uni-focused."

"OY! Am I thoisty!!!" he bellowed.

No one heard.

"OY! Am I thoisty!!!" he cried once more, cranking up the decibels.

Now people in other rooms heard, but they did not react. I guess they had grown accustomed to (read, tired of) Grandpa's demands. But the grumbling quickly changed to pleading.

"OY!!!! AM I THOISTY!!!"

It worked. "Here you go, Grandpa," offered Lisa, handing him a tall, quenching glass of lemonade, while scurrying back to the couch in the den. The book had fallen and it took her a good minute or so to find her place again. But as she gently re-entered the novel's backdrop, she heard a very familiar voice moaning from the kitchen. Yes. It was Grandpa. What could he want *now*?!

"OY! WAS I THOISTY!!!"

O.K. O.K. So I adapted an old Yiddish joke, dating back to the 50's. All right, the 30's. Somehow, that story has always occupied a soft spot in my funny bone. Poor old Grandpa...sitting alone in the kitchen. I guess he wasn't very *thoisty* after all, was he? Or maybe he was. We'll never know. But one thing we <u>do</u> know. Whether or not he was thirsty, he was certainly lonely.

You know, Passover is sooner than we think, my wife gently reminds me (every few weeks or so), and I suppose I'm thinking about Grandpa and family and things like that. But Passover really reminds me of something even more fundamental — the lost art of just "listening" to someone.

Many of us have forgotten this (myself included), but not too long ago people actually used to listen to each other. It's true! Believe it or not, people sat together, either in the park, or at a coffee shop, or on the phone. One person spoke — the other listened and then they reversed roles! That was the formula and it worked.

But those days are gone...sadly. Eye contact, empathy and just plain listening have been replaced by voice mail, email, very fast food, and "*Love to chat, but gotta.................*(voice trails off into the Palm Pilot).

What happened?

The process was a gradual one. Initially we found ourselves with less and less time for mundane activities like listening to someone else. "*So unproductive.*" Then, as video images became the modus operandi for the entire waking portion of our daily existence, we have kind of "forgotten" *how* to listen to anyone else. "*When does the film start?*" And now, I fear, if we meet someone who needs to talk, we just pity the poor soul. "*I mean...isn't that what therapists get the big bucks for?*"

Enter Passover. With all its majesty, splendor, and tradition. But amid the finest cutlery, the glimmering goblets, and the spiritual symbols galore, the Seder is really all about the art of listening.

I've heard it said that throughout the world people tell stories to their children to put them to sleep. But in Judaism, we tell our children stories to wake them up. The wine, the matzah, the *maror* (bitter herbs) are all central to our fulfillment, but our primary obligation at the Seder is simply to tell the story — the story of the miraculous events that framed our liberation from Egypt and led us on our road to Sinai. And <u>listening</u> to that story is paramount to the whole process.

The Torah, always meticulous in its written formulation, strangely prescribes for us the storytelling methodology.

> *"So that you will tell in the ears of your children and grandchildren what I wrought in Egypt" (Exodus 10:2).*

The Torah's stipulation that we speak into the "ears" of our children may have seemed somewhat superfluous for the last 131 generations or so, since Sinai. After all, to where else shall we direct our verbal communications — their hair? But today, that directive seems downright **prophetic**! There will come a time (read "now") when listening will become inefficient, forgotten, or passé. But hear the story, we must. Convey the particulars in any way you wish. Just be sure that our children are **really listening.** Speak into their ears.

Today, with our insatiable need to dissolve every nuisance facing us, however inconsequential it may be, and with our total intolerance for any discomfort whatsoever, we've lost sight of how powerful a good "listen" can actually be. Instead, we've all become "master problem-solvers" — ever-ready with several *perfect* solutions for everybody else's problems.

But by now you may have noticed...those FABULOUSLY CREATIVE solutions are rarely greeted with overwhelming enthusiasm. If you are really lucky, your illuminating insight will simply be ignored. More likely, the reaction you get will be something nestled between contempt and derision, for implying that **YOU** came up with something that **I** hadn't thought of. Hrmph!

What they really wanted when they *revealed* that problem to you was a good *listen* — attentive, compassionate, and sincere. That kind of response is always welcome. And, these days, quite unexpected. Add a dose of old-fashioned eye contact and a pinch of genuine sympathy and you'll be amazed at how ameliorative your reply will become. In other words, just replace the brain with your shoulder and watch the hearts meet.

Passover, the occasion to usher in real freedom, can also be the inauguration of a newfound commitment to give people what they *really* need most. A chance to speak. An opportunity to be heard. A comforting touch. A good *listen*.

Or maybe a glass of lemonade, too.

Bondage: Circa 2004

"Why should this Passover be different from all the other Passovers?"

Because holidays are ours to celebrate. But they are not festivals, parties or "events." The distinction lies in what we take from them. No holiday should leave us the same as we were when it began. And that takes preparation. Passover is no different.

Let us prepare.

Not long ago I was idling at a "Stop" sign and a billboard on an overpass caught my eye. It was from Citibank. I read it.

"He who dies with the most toys...is still dead! Live richly!"

I read it again. The words didn't change.

Continuing my trip, I contemplated the message I had just received. It seemed to me that the statement contained two parts:

> 1. *"He who dies with the most toys...is still dead!"*
> 2. *"Live richly!"*

Part 1 seems to make a lot of sense, perhaps bordering on the poignant. Death, being inevitable and all, should help us realize that our accumulation of "toys" is moot, at best, and pointless, at worst. As they say back home, *"You can't take it with you."*

But then the billboard does a 360. *"Live richly!"* it proclaims.

Silly me. For a minute, I thought that Citibank was expanding its investment concerns to include investing into meaningful life ventures. Might as well use our limited time here productively. But, no such luck. Instead we are implored to make loads of cash and spend it. *"Live richly!"* Indeed.

"But what's wrong with making money?" you ask. "And if I do, why shouldn't I spend it? I earned it!"

Good questions. Troubling questions. Important ones.

The way I see it, there's really nothing at all wrong with making money. I even do it myself now and then. The problem arises when making money becomes your life's goal, when living richly becomes your singular focus...your raison d'être...your daily mantra. We just seem to forget *why* we are earning money. It becomes the end instead of the means.

"But what does this have to do with Passover?" you ask.

Instead of recalling our very first liberation some 3356 years ago, let us look, for a moment, at a modern-day Exodus, of smaller proportion.

On May 24 and 25, 1991 Operation Solomon (no relation) airlifted 14,324 Jews to Israel from Ethiopia aboard 34 EL AL jets in just over 36 hours. Following its predecessors, Operations Moses and Joshua, the daring rescue mission transported this multitude of starving and unacquainted people into the strident and incredibly vibrant confines of a 20th-century metropolis. Walt Disney himself could not have imagined even a morsel of what it must have been like to escape a barbaric and malaria-dominated habitat, grab one bag of meager belongings, board a Jumbo 747 and step down on the soil of the Land of Milk, Honey, and Cell Phones.

The flock of officials, well-wishers, paparazzi, and floodlight wattage was unprecedented. But one particular encounter stands out. Reporters, desperate for headline-worthy sound bites, swarmed the new arrivals and smothered them with queries about their astonishing turn of fortune. Over and over again, with the help of translators, the guests were asked about the implausible contrasts they had just experienced. One journalist wondered what it was like to actually fly in an airplane for the first time. The response of the wide-eyed interviewee was unforgettable.

"Fly in an airplane?" he asked. "Why don't you ask me what it was like to walk down a staircase for the very first time? That was really something."

Now, no sensible person would suggest that depriving ourselves of basic conveniences and comforts of life in order to appreciate things is necessary or even laudatory. But imagine, just for a moment, living a life where walking down a staircase could be a noteworthy event. It boggles the mind. So jaded are we today that practically nothing impresses us or causes us to even take notice of the miracles of everyday life. New developments in communication, medical technology, and travel (just to name a few) are spun out faster than you can say, "microwave."

What it basically boils down to is one very simple question:

What mechanisms do you need to ensure that you truly appreciate life?

Perhaps that is what Passover 2004 is all about.

A great man (or maybe it was the "Reader's Digest") once said: *"Everyone seems to be searching for the city of happiness. What they don't realize is that it can only be found in the state of mind."*

When we stop to think about it, we all know this is true. Problem is, we just don't stop to think about it. Now, more than ever, we seek fortune instead of satisfaction, fame instead of self-respect, success instead of contentment. We get so caught up in accumulating the most "toys," that we lose sight of our true goals. We forget that success is getting what you want; happiness is wanting what you get.

Our friends from Ethiopia were so deprived that a simple walk down a staircase became a fantasy come true. And our ancestors in Egypt lived under such brutal and heartless conditions, for much of 210 years, that some sun-baked matzah and a march into the desert became cause for a fevered celebration. I guess it all depends on where you are coming from.

This Passover, as we sit at the Seder, we must each take a deep hard look at ourselves and ask: *"Where am I coming from?"*

If your true answer is, *"I come from the land of Citibank, I live richly,"* and that remains your essential life goal, you may have trouble feeling the joy of liberation and the thrill of what freedom really means. In millennia past we were slaves to the Pharahos; today we are slaves to the holy dollar. Is there really much of a difference?

If, on the other hand, you prepare yourself to appreciate every tinge of life's incredible beauty and every wonder that surrounds us, that remarkable sensation we call "freedom" will wash over you like a great wave of exhilaration and will help steer your ship into that sea of happiness that is your state of mind. Think about it. No one ever died regretting that he had not spent more time in the office.

This Passover, with the right preparation, we can transform our internal bondage into an introspective process that brings us to new heights of awareness and gratitude. Unlike the international scorn and enmity that reluctantly and relentlessly chain us together as a People, these are constructive themes that can truly unite us and give us strength to fulfill our promise for eternity.

It is with this realization that we can then write our own billboard:

> *"He who lives with the most appreciation will never be a slave again! Live freely!"*

Now that's what I call emancipation.

Happy Passover.

Packing for Yom Kippur
Leave the Blame at Home

I look at the pictures, just like you do, and wonder in total disbelief.

"Is that a car under all that water, or is it a boat?"

"For how long were those people stuck on their own roofs?"

"Didn't they realize that those levees weren't strong enough?"

"That couldn't be the SUPERDOME, could it?"

"For heaven's sake, why didn't they get out while they could?"

Katrina, perhaps the greatest natural disaster ever to hit American soil, has claimed countless casualties, destroyed the lives of every "fortunate" survivor, and wreaked havoc with our pristine and invincible national psyche.

And while the corpses were yet damp and the downtown intersections still deluged, the obligatory finger-pointing could not wait. Read the press. Hear the news. Watch the circus. Today it's the Mayor, tomorrow it's Bush.

"The engineers were amateurs."

"G-d has spoken."

"FEMA was totally inept."
"The Governor should resign."
"It was a city of depravity."
"Ariel Sharon is the source of all things evil."

And so it goes. Scapegoats are vilified and proletarians are suddenly promoted to pundits. And all the while, funerals and burials become daily fare as hundreds of thousands wonder when Houston became a suburb of New Orleans.

A storm from hell has ravaged our coastline and permanently crumbled multitudinous lives. And what is our primary and immediate response? Recriminations and blame. Sure, it's important to know what went wrong in the rescue efforts. We must learn from our mistakes. But couldn't *The Fault Show* have waited just a bit, so we could mourn and bury and regroup first? I suppose that's what feelings of helplessness can often cause.

Of course, blame is not an unfamiliar concept to the Jews. Two thousand plus years of Crusades, pogroms, holocausts and expulsions can do that to a People.

But blame, for all its damaging implications, also connotes responsibility — personal, familial, and communal. And Jews, especially during these Days of Awe, embrace this concept of taking responsibility for our actions and our passivity — even our thoughts and feelings. We take pride as we take stock. Painful as the process is, we almost savor the cleansing feeling that washes over us as the Yom Kippur sunset escorts our final petitions, leading us to ultimate atonement.

Sometimes, however, in our zeal to achieve rectification, we distort this requisite sense of accountability in a damaging way. Self-blame can easily be transformed into undue shame and humiliation. Guilt feelings, the kind necessary to pave the road to self-improvement, often become much more than that. They dominate our spirit. We punish ourselves in ways that can bruise and impair our sense of self. Perfection is mistaken for purification. I'm not sure that is what Yom Kippur is really about.

The venerable 19th-century sage, Rabbi Yisrael Salanter, once asked an obvious question and offered a penetrating response. "Why did G-d choose to position Yom Kippur *after* Rosh Hashanah? Yom Kippur is the Day of Atonement; Rosh Hashanah celebrates

G-d's dominion over the universe and the unique role that we, His Chosen People, play in that cosmos. Wouldn't it be far more logical to *enter* that glorified state *after* we have undergone the spiritual refinement of Yom Kippur?

It is actually very much the contrary, explained the wise rabbi. We don't need to be totally purified to attain the exalted status of membership in the Army of the Supreme. We achieve that holy order just by being who we are — yes, with all of our blemishes and imperfections and weaknesses. It's called being human.

"But shouldn't we, at least, *try* to perfect ourselves wherever possible," you ask. Of course. It is, in fact, precisely that effort that brings us to higher and higher levels of compassion, understanding and holiness. But when perfection becomes our *only* acceptable goal and when falling short of that causes *unhealthy* guilt, and *crippling* self-blame and despondence, we have clearly gone too far.

Life, as we've all been told so many times, is indeed a trip. And when we travel by plane, each one of us undergoes intense scrutiny. And as we meander our way through the strains of airport security, we inch closer and closer to the Big Moment — when we must come face to face with the dreaded but essential X-Ray Machine and Metal Detector. We are asked to place everything we own on the conveyor belt so that each and every item can be carefully examined. We "know" we are entering a "holy place" because often times we must even remove our shoes.

And then, in single file, we march through the machine hoping, perhaps praying, that the dreaded alarm doesn't sound, signaling that we have been selected for even closer examination.

But even if that bell does go off, it doesn't mean that you won't get on the plane. You may just be asked to leave an item behind or to explain why you need to carry something with you. Yes, even with imperfections you can still get a boarding pass.

And so it is on Yom Kippur. We wind our way through the year and finally reach the Big Day, when we must come face to face with the A-mighty. Everything we've done is carefully scrutinized and evaluated. We have even left our shoes at home.

And then, as we say in our holy prayers, all of mankind passes before G-d like members of the flock approaching the spiritual metal detector. Like sheep walking in single file before their owner, we pass under His staff and hold our breath, awaiting His decree.

We close our eyes and pray that the dreaded alarm remain silent and we are granted passage for another year.

But we needn't be flawless to get that boarding pass — no one is. We may be asked to leave certain sins or faults behind or to explain why we failed to reach our potential this year. These are important questions — questions that we should be asking ourselves.

But the G-d of Mercy understands each and every one of us. He sees through our baggage with perfect x-ray vision. He knows our intentions and he knows our pretensions. He judges our level of sincerity and takes our struggles into full account. And all He really wants is our full effort — complete, earnest, and heartfelt.

Yes, Yom Kippur is a day of breast-beating, tears, and unparalleled reverence. But all of that is enhanced when we remain in full cognizance of G-d's unconditional love for His children.

This year, when you finish your last-minute packing, leave the dagger at home. Pack a really good prayer-book, some very sincere resolutions, and lots of tissues.

And have a nice trip.

May we all arrive safely.

The Mystery of 1964

*T*he year was 1964.

The World's Fair opened in Flushing Park. Some far-out location called Vietnam dominated the news. The Mets played their first game at Shea Stadium. And Dallas' "grassy knoll" was a familiar term in the American lexicon. Those were the head-lines that danced in the mind of a 12-year-old New York City boy. That boy was me.

Life was good, I recall. Lots of friends, loving parents, "Leave It to Beaver," my trusty black outfielder's glove, and an older brother to show me the ropes. What could be bad?

I suppose that in my own naïve way, I was decidedly unaware that there was anything special or distinctive about being a child of Holocaust survivors. Everything seemed so very normal. In fact, it was.

As it turns out, many of my baby-boomer friends were of similar ilk. Their parents had also either spent years in camps of various disrepute or had barely escaped the clutches of catastrophe on more than one occasion, and lived to tell about it. But looking back, I find it odd that we were all so oblivious to our unique lineage. We never compared notes, never wondered if we were "different," never discussed how our parents' suffering and deprivation may have affected us, never seemed to even notice that we were members of this proud yet sad club. Not in class, not in the synagogue, not even during sleepovers when the darkness sheltered our fragility. Never.

And I guess that's how our folks really wanted it to be. *"Blend in, be normal, forget the past, look ahead..."* read their unspoken banner of postwar parenting. I suppose that they had had quite enough of being part of an exclusive grouping of any kind. Being special does have its disadvantages, you know. No. Now was the time to de-emphasize our distinctions and hope for a brighter, or at least, normal tomorrow.

And if this society of kids of survivors was, in fact, bent on changing its moniker to *"Club Inconspicuous,"* then surely I was prime candidate for president. Despite having spent over 3 years in the torture cavities of Puskow, Mielec, Wieliczka, Flossenberg, Leitmeritz, Dachau, and Kaufering, my father, of blessed memory, never ever uttered a single word to us about the butchery and carnage he witnessed there daily. It was as if life on this planet somehow began in 1947 — when he arrived in the United States.

It's not like we didn't know that "something" dreadful had happened. We saw the "KL" that had been eternalized on his wrist, we knew about the huge bump he carried beneath his black, shiny yarmulke, and we cried when we were awoken by his terrifying nocturnal screams and tremors. Oh, we knew. But the horror was just too ghastly to verbalize. The "pink elephant" could not be spoken about. The children had to be protected.

The only exception to this pact of silence was when Daddy took me to Riverside Park just about every Shabbos afternoon. It was there that Paul and Danny and Joey and Eli and the rest of my fellow club members would join me for a weekly Freeze-tag or Ring-o-leevio game. But it wasn't long before I noticed that while we were busy darting and leaping on and off base, and releasing our preadolescent tensions, our fathers formed an enclave of their own.

The spirit and animation of their discussions always seemed a trifle inappropriate, until one day I happened by within earshot and discovered that it was there that they swapped horror stories, never to be forgotten. It seems that every week for 2 hours or more, these valiant heroes turned the clock back 20-plus years and compared their dreaded experiences, to relive and recount what their eyes had witnessed and their hearts had endured. It was a support group of the most therapeutic kind.

The mystery unfolded that summer. Like every year, I was safely ensconced in my home away from home — my summer camp near

New Paltz, New York — when I received a letter from home. This itself was a rather common occurrence in the pre-email decade of the 60's. Preposterous as it sounds, people (especially parents with kids in camp) would actually sit down at a table or a desk, pick up a ball point pen (I believe that Bic had just entered the scene) and some blank paper (ruled or unruled), and communicate news from home and abroad. The paper would subsequently be inserted in an envelope which was then addressed, sealed, stamped and brought to a mailing receptacle. Days later, the letter invariably arrived. Amazing.

After Mommy's usual exhortations to wear a sweater at night, learn how to swim, and eat my veggies, Daddy would customarily also take a turn — adding a few obligatory greetings in his forced, but loving, broken English. But this letter was different. No message from Daddy. He would never write very much anyway, but I always looked for his unfinished, yet ever so sincere message of missing me and loving me. It wasn't there. At 12 years old, that struck a chord.

When I couldn't speak to Daddy on my weekly call home, an explanation had to be tendered. *"Oh,"* Mom stumbled, *"he went to Israel to attend your cousin's wedding."* Plausible enough. But not for 1964...and not for my father...and not without months of preparatory excitement and anticipation. I knew it didn't smell right, but hey, I was only 12 and heavily involved in Color War and batting leadoff. Priorities, you know. I let it slide.

And so it remained — a minor mystery — tempered somewhat by Daddy's return home two weeks later, armed with wedding pictures, a silver candelabra for Mommy, and Jerusalem trinkets for the boys. Perhaps I was wrong.

Fast forward nearly 40 years. Daddy is with us — but in spirit and memory now, and big brother Izzy has grown fascinated with Daddy's earlier years in particular and our family genealogy in general. In frenetic fashion, Izzy assumes the identity of an impassioned world-class detective, gripped with the unyielding determination to shed light on the questions we never dared ask.

- *What were Daddy's formative years like?*
- *Where did the family come from?*
- *What were they known for?*

- *Where were they before and during the war?*

- *How many were killed?*

- *Who else, if any, survived?*

- *How?*

- *Did Daddy begin a family before the war?*

- *What happened to them?*

- *What horrors did he witness?*

- *How did he stay alive?*

- *...and where did he go in July of 1964?*

Izzy traveled...to Poland, to Israel...and he asked questions. He read. He surfed. He called. He wrote. He wondered. He dreamed. He interviewed. He cried. He uncovered. He discovered. He was stymied, exhausted, confused, elated, obstructed, and jubilant. Sometimes all at the same time. But most of all, he was driven. Driven by a passion to know, to understand, and to connect.

And he found answers — at least some of them — that help to fill part of the void we had grappled with for so many years. The "research" is ongoing and more answers may still be forthcoming. Some questions will never be answered and perhaps that is how it should be, but the mystery of 1964 is no longer. A short time ago he received a correspondence from the Provincial Court of Bochum, Germany. In it was a transcript dated July 21, 1964. It was Daddy's verbatim testimony at a trial for Nazi War Criminals.

> *"In April of 1942 I was arrested by the Jewish police. I had heard that the Gestapo ordered the Jewish police to arrest young, strong, able-bodied boys and men. The police had a list of about 100 names, and I was one of them."*

Daddy then identified Nazis, unfamiliar to most: Johann, Labitzke, Rouenhoff, Bornhold, Brock. It seems that all of them must have been on trial. I trembled as I read on. I can hear his gentle voice speaking.

> *"The prison cell was so overcrowded that we had no room to stretch out at night.*
>
> *"Before shipping out we were assembled in the prison courtyard and had to line up in three rows. I stood in the*

middle row. About 8 to 10 Jews stepped forward and declared themselves sick. One Jew, for example, had bloody feet."

It was incredible to read the words my father had said, describing events that I never could have heard him say directly. It was a glimpse into a corridor that had been closed off to all of us as long as he lived. His next words merged the unspeakable with staggering historical irony.

"A second Jew dropped his pants and showed his hernia. These sick people were told to step aside. Hamann pointed to the wall and they went there.

"I saw these SS people from Puskow approach the sick Jews and stand near them. Then I heard Hamann calling out 'Fire,' and the SS men fired. The 8 to 10 sick Jews were shot to death."

My face dropped. Reading the eyewitness account of my very own, tender loving father bearing witness to watching Jews being shot to death is an experience that defies description. But learning that the Nazi in charge of this particular bloodbath was Hamann, the namesake of the villainous protagonist of the Purim story, whose intent was to exterminate masses of Jews, was truly mind-boggling.

"I am the only survivor of those sent to the Puskow Labor Camp."

And with that, Daddy's testimony ended.

My understanding is that these Gestapo thugs all received sentences of life imprisonment. Whether they actually served them full term is unknown to me.

Daddy, I have spent many adult years wondering what really happened to you before 1947. I believe it is something that all children of survivors would do well to look into. But looking back now, and knowing that I am now privy to but a speck of the terror you lived through, I say thank you. Thank you for making me president of *Club Inconspicuous.* Your loving shield was a blanket of normalcy for two little boys who love you now even more than we ever did.

Life was good, I recall.

You made it that way.

From Station
to Station

*C*all me a fanatic. "An extremist," perhaps. Go ahead. I won't blame you. I might even join you. What I've done warrants a designation of that sort. And yet I wouldn't want it any other way.

Allow me to explain. Today marks three months since I last listened to the radio. That's right. No news. No sports. No music ("light" or any other kind). No talk shows. No commercials. No public service announcements. No traffic and weather together... or separately. In short — no static. No noise. Just quiet. Quiet at home. Quiet in the office. Quiet in the car. Quiet.

Quiet? Quiet in New York City? Can it be? Can the noise really vanish? No. Not entirely. But it can be filtered. And it can be productive. AND entertaining. And stimulating. And pleasant.

∽ THE GENESIS

My "discovery" of this most dramatic utilization of my *bechirah chafshis* (free will) came totally without warning. It was *Shabbos Shuvah* and the words leaped out of his *derashah* (sermon), not unlike a "special bulletin" interrupting a "regularly scheduled broadcast." "Isn't your time and attention worth more than whatever is blaring on the radio?"

For some reason, I took the question seriously, though it was probably meant rhetorically. I took it personally, not philosophically. "Isn't it," I asked myself?

"Do I really gain much, or anything, from the decibels of drivel being aimed at my eardrum medulla, wallet, and *neshamah?*"

Can life possibly proceed without knowledge of immediate and detailed reports and analyses of every idiosyncratic phenomenon of every sector of the globe?!

Will I cease to exist without political acumen, disaster tolls, investment expertise, talk show hosts, tips on tree pruning, current hockey injuries, Frank Perdue, the eminent SHADOW TRAFFIC, and the ever-so-exalted FIVE DAY FORECAST? I had to find out.

☜ IN THE BEGINNING...

I began immediately after Shabbos. "One day at a time," I told myself. "Let's see what develops."

The project intrigued me almost immediately. The first thing I became aware of was how much radio I *used* to listen to. Not really listen, perhaps, but *on* nevertheless. "Background noise," we call it. As if my effervescent, never docile family didn't provide enough background noise. And yet there I was — instinctively, even habitually, on "day one," reaching out for the magical "on" switch.

"*Vatishlach es amasah,*" I thought. Pharaoh's daughter, Basya, *lehavdil*, also extended her arm in instinctive fashion, to save the abandoned and crying infant and future leader of *Klal Yisrael*. Had she allowed logic to invade her intent, explains Reb Chaim Shmulevitz, the great distance between her and the cradle in distress would have certainly precluded any attempt of rescue. But Hashem performs miracles when our instincts are so pure and well intentioned. A helping hand was transformed into an extension of Providence that altered history forever.

My outstretched arm had far less imposing ramifications. Mankind, as we know it, would not be eternally transformed by my experimental abstinence. But if we are true believers of *bishvili nivra ha'olam* (the universe was created for me), "my world" might never again be the same. Perhaps Hashem had a meager miracle available for these private times, too. Slowly I drew my hand back ...and smiled. Insignificant? I think not.

↷ OUT OF THE CLOSET

The days went by and the experiment continued. After four days, I revealed to my wife my "silly" little foray into the world of isolation. I wanted to be sure it was real. She didn't laugh. It was real.

Information infiltrated. News entered via *The Wall Street Journal,* the only newspaper I can bring into my home without blushing — not AM or FM. Music was selected from tapes — some long buried. Weather reports arrived with alarming accuracy for a change — I opened my window. Insights and analyses were now gleaned from speeches of *gedolim* (Torah giants), both current and past, recorded and live. And the hockey injuries continued to mount — I can only assume.

Slowly I confided in friends...carefully selected. Most of them were surprised. "Not even TRAFFIC REPORTS???"

Some showed concern. "You didn't make a *neder* (vow), I hope."

A few were jealous. "It won't last, you know."

No one required oxygen.

One supporter suggested a goal, to reinforce my resolve. "Hold out at least until *Hoshana Rabbah,"* he said (two weeks from the start). A new rendering, perhaps, to *"Kol mevasser, mevasser v'omer"* (the voice of the herald, heralds and proclaims).

Yom Tov ended, but the static blackout was showing fresh legs. Not unlike the recovering compulsive smoker who eventually discovers that his body no longer craves nicotine, I, too, was doing fine, thank you. I noted no more episodes of instinctive radio "outreach," and less and less curiosity about events that very recently seemed indispensable and spellbinding. My challenging enterprise was actually getting easy. *"Haba l'taher m'saiyin oso —* One who comes to be purified receives special (heavenly) assistance" (*Shabbos* 104a).

↷ THE HOME STRETCH

The human species is a creature of habit. We become so accustomed to doing things in a certain way that we frequently do not consider that there might actually be alternatives. When this *hergel* (regularity) sets in, we become more robot than man, and our daily routine becomes just that — routine. The *navi Yeshayahu* (29:13) refers to this phenomenon as *"mitzvas anashim melumadah,"* performing mitzvos with oblivious regularity. But the same holds true for everything we do, whether they be mitzvos or otherwise. We tend to forget *what* we are doing and *why* we are doing it. It is then that man becomes an actual prisoner, locked into a system of habitual behavior that dictates virtually every step he takes and fastens him to a gestalt of trancelike conduct.

On a recent visit to Eretz Yisrael, I was fortunate to have taken a tour of the current excavations being conducted on the southern side of the *Har HaBayis* (Temple Mount). While ambling down the numerous steps that meander their way through *mikvaos* (ritual baths) and ruins, I couldn't help noticing that each step of stone seemed to vary from the previous one, both in dimension and in depth. Negotiating the hike down was rendered rather cumbersome by the inconsistencies in the construction. "Lousy architect," I quipped with irreverence to our tour guide.

"Not at all," he responded.

"Quite the contrary," he added. "Have you ever heard of the concept of *mitzvas anashim melumadah*?"

I understood. The Temple contractors, with their keen wisdom, realized that even something as sacred as a visit to the *Beis HaMikdash* was in jeopardy of becoming routine to many, especially those who came often. (Notice the similarity between the words *"hergel"* and "regular"?) Constructing the steps in unequal proportion would compel the visitor to concentrate and reflect on each and every step he took into the *makom kadosh* (holy place), and think about why he was there. Brilliant.

∽ CRASHING THROUGH THE CLUTCHES OF "HERGEL"

Many of you are, in all likelihood, a lot like me. A radio addict, by habit. You cannot imagine life without it. The media itself has ingrained in us the concept of the "requirement" to know "all the news, all the time." But crashing through the clutches of *hergel* can have extraordinary effects on one's *tzelem Elokim* (G-dly image) [see *all* the major *sifrei mussar*]. And the venerable radio could be a great place to begin that assault.

Yes. Reason must prevail. *Sheviras hamiddos* (breaking one's habits) need not require that you flee any department store that happens to be playing a radio on its sound system. Nor must you hang up on your travel agent whenever he places you on "hold."

And yes. There are more important issues for us to grapple with — as a People, in our communities, in our families, and even in ourselves. But our Torah society has already made huge strides in the anti-television campaign, and clearly every elevation of *kedushah* can only help.

So call me a fanatic. Go ahead. But first try it for a week. Or maybe just a day. If you find quitting difficult, beware. You just might be hooked on radio.

One final note of caution: Tuning *out* your radio could become habit forming too. For me, the habit is three months and counting.

So give away those 22 minutes; you could get back your world.

The Day After...

Can you write a song without music?
Can you construct a house without concrete, wood, and steel?
Can you build a relationship without feelings?
And can you write an article without words?

*T*oday is September 12, 2001, forever to be known as "The Day After...," and my soul compels me to write about yesterday. But it isn't easy without words. The words, you see, have not yet been created to properly depict events and emotions that no one dreamed he would ever see or feel.

And yet, millions around the world listen to media analysts, scan the radio waves, read the tabloids, and surf the web...searching, exploring, desperately hunting for the description that will connect with their sentiment or soothe their pain.

Which nouns and adjectives do you relate to?

"Shock?"

"Devastation?"

"Senseless?"

"Unspeakable?"

Does "horrifying" suffice or would "ghastly" come closer to home?

Perhaps the prophet Jeremiah, in his epic requiem, *"Eichah,"* said it best. In lamenting the fall of the Jews and Jerusalem over 2400 years ago, he used the simple word, "Alas!" It is more of an utterance than a word. It is a cry. A wail. A guttural expression that goes beyond the limits of any finite definition. Real words just don't capture what has happened to our world. "Alas!"

⌾ ACTION

There are those whose intense pain may lead them to the feeling that speaking about action, in the wake of immeasurable grief and bereavement, may be insensitive or even disrespectful. I can understand that, but I cannot agree. "Response" is not a contradiction to loss. It is its evolvement.

In truth, if ever there were a time when the saying, **"actions speak louder than words,"** was appropriate, this would seem to be it.

Certainly the actions of the heroes in the ongoing Herculean rescue effort speak volumes about the value of human life...and death. And certainly the actions of the thousands who waited in lines for hours to donate blood speak clearly about caring for one's fellow man or woman. And certainly the military response that must surely follow will speak loudly about the lessons that need to be learned and taught.

But cataclysmic events also call for actions of a different strain. Actions of a very personal nature.

I'm not alone in feeling numb, while I struggle and contemplate what it is I could possibly do now. Despite my full realization that language will be totally inadequate in any attempt to encapsulate the enormity of the calamitous nightmare that has occurred, I find I am no different from most. I too scour the media in my own frantic pursuit of some kind of literary balm. The journey is fruitless, yet fixating, at the same time. I suppose this is all part of the "healing process," as they taught us in graduate school.

But one observation emerges. After all the pundits have concluded their conjecturing and meandering, they seem to land on the same finish line — more or less. No matter how you size up the particulars, they say, one conclusion is clear — "Our lives will never be the same again."

And then something strange happened. The *more* I read it, the *less* I understood it! "Our lives will never be the same again."

What does that mean? Is it something positive or negative? Are they referring to a state of fear and chronic insecurity or to a dazed impetus toward resolution and self-improvement?

∽ SOUND THE ALARM

Shocking events of mammoth proportion contain within them colossal potential for serious contemplation. Nothing gets you moving faster than the rage of a five-alarm fire, which might be why G-d sends one in the first place!

But the *real* shock is what happens afterwards — *after* the blaze is doused, the smoke has cleared, and the embers cease to smolder. More often than not, the fire is gone. Daily life resumes — as well it should. But when it does, it often extinguishes the inspiration and passion that could have brought about <u>real</u> and <u>lasting</u> changes. What seemed so important just a few days ago suddenly appears trivial, grueling, or just out of reach. The event, so traumatic and packed with vitality, actually fades into the permanent recycle bin. The "wake-up" button becomes the "snooze" button.

Yes, there are exceptions — plenty of them. But most of us somehow fall prey to the clutches of complacency. The promises fade and the perseverance all but vanishes. We forget...we deny...we rationalize — and sadly, we stay the same.

There are no magical ways to avoid this plunge into neutral gear. The conviction necessary to forge ahead must come from within. Only a relentless surge of zeal and enthusiasm can forestall the avalanche of resignation. It takes real muscle to remain steadfast in your new resolve. It also helps to start as close to the event as possible. Sometimes a great start can give you the momentum you need.

I can't tell you the specifics of what these days of apocalypse should catapult you to do. As mentioned earlier, the action you need to take is very personal. Only <u>you</u> know, deep down, the changes you need to make.

I <u>can</u> tell you one thing. No matter how dreadful and alarming the current situation may seem, even a catastrophe as virulent as this one is also subject to the very same perils of complacency.

The analysts are wrong. The tragedy today is not that "Our lives will never be the same again." The tragedy is that, in all likelihood, our lives will actually be **very much the same again.**

You know what to do.

Do it now. You may never get the chance again.

Alas.

Waiting in the Waiting Room

What do you do while you wait for the doctor in the waiting room?

We all go to the doctor and the dentist — at least, we should. And we all wait — often for too long. But how do we spend those nervous moments?

Next time you're there, take a look around. The possibilities seem endless.

If it's your first visit to a particular specialist, you may very well engage in trying to figure out who the doctor actually is. The "secret passage" leading to the examining and consultation rooms swings open many times during your wait, and you might find yourself peering inside to catch a glimpse of the staff in an attempt to identify the doctor. It isn't easy nowadays, since the traditional *white coat* is often eschewed in today's "normalized" medical settings...probably to make the game a bit more challenging. Patients can even be seen playing a variation of musical chairs, sometimes resorting to switching seats as they vie for the best angle in scanning the scene.

Reading the minds of fellow waiting-room patients is another frequent practice. You judge the purpose of their visits based on age, manifest tension, posture, and questions they ask the receptionist — and conclude whether they are here for something acute, chronic, or imagined.

Saying *Tehillim* (Psalms) is certainly a praiseworthy endeavor, but magazine perusal is the standard waiting-room fare. Unfortunately, the magazine selection frequently defies reason and you find yourself having to choose between an ancient copy of *National Review* with a bewildered Michael Dukakis on the cover, *Golf Digest*, *Kidney Quarterly,* and the like.

A newer trend has patients on cell phones, loudly instructing their children how to defrost exotic vegetables, arguing with their service carrier about roaming charges, or planning vacation excursions with anyone who will listen. *Annoying* is an understatement.

But a recent waiting-room experience of my own shed a new perspective on this seemingly mundane subject matter.

It seems that marketing pundits have determined that depriving oneself of video stimulation for even a short span of time might be hazardous to one's health. And so, many waiting rooms (and barber shops and even banks) now house TVs or VCRs for our viewing pleasure while we wait. No matter how hard we try to escape its influence, the entertainment industry perseveres. At times, regularly scheduled programs are shown and sometimes infomercials hawking specific medications, treatment facilities, or exercise regimens are presented.

Some months ago, there was a TV commercial. I knew immediately it was a commercial since the decibel level seemed to suddenly double.

> *"Do you remember this song?" the announcer beckoned.*
>
> *"'We're goin' to America...we're goin' to America... TODAY!'*
>
> *"Turn the clock back and hear the newly digitally mastered tracks you've loved so much — 24 top-of-the-chart hits all on one extraordinary CD."*

I smiled. This little commercial was designed to transport people back to a time of longing days and syrupy innocence. "Isn't nostalgia wonderful?" I mused.

But suddenly, out of nowhere, the announcer floored me with his final desperate pitch.

> *"Order now...operators are standing by...don't miss this incredible opportunity to get 24 of his most IMPORTANT contributions!"*

My head winced in incredulity. Did he say *"IMPORTANT"* contributions? And then, right on cue, the broadcaster repeated it — just for my sake.

Now, call me sacrilegious, if you want. I'm well aware that, to many people out there, the singer is a hero, an icon, a celebrity of immeasurable musical proportion. But would anyone seriously consider *Song Sung Blue* an "important" contribution? His greatest fan, I'd bet, would hesitate to deem *I Am...I Said* even remotely "important."

I'd guess that even the singer himself (born 63 years ago as Noah Kaminsky) might be a tad embarrassed by the designation *"Important"* being placed next to his songs.

I took a swift glimpse around. My eyes surveyed the waiting room. Soon I'd be called in for my stress test. "Routine," said my internist. He was right, I assured myself. But glancing at the anxious couple in their 70's across from me, I doubted that their visit was, in any way, ordinary or routine. Nor did the frail white-haired woman sitting alone next to me look especially healthy or relaxed. No. This was a serious place, this waiting room. *Important* — even life-and-death — considerations filled the minds of these patients.

Now roused by the stark contrast between the truly important matters that filled this anteroom of apprehension and the preposterous description of golden-oldies as being *important* too, my thoughts shifted to the sublime question of what I considered to be really important.

Within moments, my mind was bombarded by topics of potential significance — G-d, health, family, religion, relationships, life-goals, priorities, Israel, world peace, education, purpose, livelihood, creativity, food (food?), and many many others. This was "heavy" stuff, I thought. But it's good stuff...appropriate contemplation for a waiting room.

Just a few minutes earlier, the nurse had handed me a medical history questionnaire and a clipboard. There were a hundred "yes" or "no" questions that I had to answer. I never knew so many serious diseases, conditions, and symptoms even existed. I recalled that the entire form took me less than 3 minutes to fill out. What a shame. The human organism is so very complex. There are so many things that could go wrong. I should have paused every single time I checked the "no" box, and uttered *"Thank G-d."* Again, good use of waiting-room time.

Then I remembered an item I had read several years ago about a gubernatorial candidate who was asked why he thought he had lost the election. His answer was downright startling, and I never forgot it.

> *"I was being interviewed one day," [he] said, "and I was asked what I thought was the single most important thing to teach our children. I believe that the answer I gave cost me the election. I said that the most important thing to teach our children is that one day they will die."*

Apparently, he felt, people were just not ready to hear such blunt advice. And they punished him with their ballot.

I think it not coincidental that this particular story suddenly popped into my waiting-room reflections. Whether or not I agreed with what the candidate said is moot. But not losing sight of one's mortality can inarguably be termed "important."

Strange. The incongruity of an entertainer's songs being termed "important" had led me to some *truly* important places — compassion, consideration of life's priorities, appreciation, and the mortality of man.

I believe it was Bertrand Russell who once said, *"Man would sooner die than think; in fact, he often does."*

Thinking. Now, that's something we all can do in the waiting room...if we dare.

In *Ethics of the Fathers* (4:21) we are taught:

> *"Rabbi Yaakov says: This world is like an antechamber before the World to Come. Prepare yourself in the antechamber so that you may enter the banquet hall."*

All of us have seats in this giant waiting room that we call Planet Earth. Someday our names will be called.

What will you be occupied with?

From Station to Station
— Revisited

You remember me.

Of course you remember me. I'm the guy you laughed at almost two years ago. I'm the guy you called "a fanatic." "I'm sure he means well," you said about me, "but he's taken an accelerated move to the right. He's gone just a bit too far!"

I'm the guy who stopped listening to the radio. And I asked you to do the same. Or at least to try it.

*A*t the time of my last writing, I had been three months into my media abstinence and I reported no withdrawal pains, or identifiably injurious side effects. (I counted an elevation of *kedushah* as something rather positive.) And the responses I received varied from those of you who admired my determination, to those who mocked my excessive isolation, to those who were flat-out confused.

Well, what started out as an experiment in self-control has become (at least thus far) a treasured gestalt of the everyday life of this *galus* Jew. To quote myself, "One final note of caution: Tuning out your radio COULD become habit forming too!" My prediction came true...at least for me. I'm currently holding at 22 months and still counting. No, I did not enter this crusade thinking it would last a year and a half or longer. But I have enjoyed it. Immensely, I might add. And like so many new Daf Yomi recruits, I just take one day at a time and ingest the purity.

∞ THINGS HAVE CHANGED

So why do I visit you again now? Simply to apprise you of my progress? To restate my petition for you to join the media-free association? Hardly. My purpose for this return call is to advise you of a significant change in status of my "call to action." An "upgrade," if you will. From "code blue" to "code red."

At the time my initial article was published, this proposal could have been filed under the heading, "Betterment of Self," or perhaps *"Middas Chassidus."* But, my friends, nineteen months is a long time. A very long time. And much has changed. File this very same proposal today under, "DANGER AHEAD!," or, "Not Suitable for Children (or adults)," or, *"Tzeniyus* 101." That innocent looking radio, in nearly every room in your home, is wreaking potential peril to every pair of ears in your *mikdash me'at.* Code red has arrived.

I am, of course, referring to the recent allegations of depravity of our commander-in-chief. Never before, even here in the most permissive of all cultures, has such open indecency been bandied about and broadcast without so much as a second glance or hesitation. Indeed, the past couple of months have been witness to yet a new underside in media indulgence. Graphic, unfiltered, scandalous accusations have become daily fare for "responsible reporting" to the now anesthetized American public. "Impropriety in the White House!" And all in the guise of "news" — whether it is truly "fit to print (or listen to)" or not. It no longer matters. "The truth must be uncovered" and "the show must go on" have suddenly become synonymous. No matter what the damage to whatever remnants of decency we may possibly have left.

I have, in recent weeks, found it difficult to mask my anonymity when, on more than one occasion, friends have innocently commented on the sordid exposure with, "It's gotten so you can hardly even listen to the radio anymore!" And, "My kids were in the car and I realized that I better shut the radio. And I was only listening to the news!"

Mind you, my original outcry against Marconi's legacy had very little to do with the dangers of tuning in to the all too prevalent vulgarities and wanton innuendo that permeate the dial. Programming of that ilk was, not too long ago, easily identifiable and therefore quite avoidable. Rather, it was the addictive quality of needing to stay totally "informed" that presented the true danger to our *neshamos.* Radio abstinence thus became a viable vehicle to help in our struggle to defeat the evils of *hergel* (oblivious regularity).

☜ A HEAVENLY REMINDER

But the stakes have been raised. The enemy is now camouflaged in the haven of the headlines and our vulnerability is enormous. A classic reminder of Yaakov Avinu's supplication, *"Hatzileini nah me'yad achi, me'yad Eisav* — Save me from the hands of my brother, from the hands of Eisav" (*Bereishis* 32:12). Many commentators note that Yaakov Avinu is giving fair warning for all generations that the dangers of evil can be presented directly, as *Eisav,* or indirectly, disguised as *achi,* my brother.

Far more potent are the hazards of contamination when they are cloaked in a sealed container marked "parve," than when the ingredients clearly announce the inclusion of lard.

> *Who, but the most fanatical, could ever argue that there was anything "really wrong" with keeping abreast of world events? Isn't ignorance the real adversary? Shouldn't we make it our business to be informed of the news that affects our daily lives? Wasn't the creation of "all news radio" and CNN et al. really a gift from the Ribbono Shel Olam to the Torah world?*

A gift? I think not. A test? Perhaps. How much diversion do we actually need? This is a question that each of us must honestly confront especially today, when the spiritual cost of keeping informed is so alarmingly high.

We all know that nothing in life is coincidental. But it may be time for another reminder. Maybe all the furor on Pennsylvania Avenue is another carefully orchestrated plan by the *true* Commander-in-Chief, designed precisely for us, His People. Maybe He saw the need to assist those who wish to ascribe to a higher calling, so he "raised the bar" a little. So we can reach. Climb higher. Cast aside the distractions. Concentrate more on our goals and aspirations. Without the perilous forces of *hergel* undermining our mission. So He raised the stakes...to test us and to help us. He put the "lard" in the headlines!

Shall we bury our heads in the sand? Return to the ghetto? Create Israeli-style "sealed rooms" of informational insulation? Retreat to the cave?

You know what? I'm no longer sure that we can afford *not* to. I *am* sure that it is **worth a try.**

For Just One Week...

I'd like to abolish the expression "I don't know." Deprived of these three words of simplistic surrender, we would be forced to actually THINK more, guess more, and commit when we're afraid to.

...I'd like to pray as if my life really depended on it...because it does.

...I'd like to eat whatever I please — without even having to think about it — and then find that I've lost 12 pounds.

...I'd like to meet and pick the minds of the ten greatest Jews alive today. I'd ask them great philosophical questions and maybe even understand their answers. I'd ask them what it was that made them who they are. I'd ask them who their true role models were and are. And I'd ask them very personal questions, for all the right reasons, without having to fear that I was trespassing.

...I'd like to offer genuine constructive criticism to my loved ones without having to wonder if I was hurting them.

...I'd like to welcome *their* constructive criticism of *me* and have me accept it without feeling slighted or rejected...too much.

...I'd love to see the friends that I cherish who are so ill, be able to enjoy life like they used to.

...I'd like to read 90 percent of my ever-growing *must read* pile. I am convinced that ensconced in that "holy" collection are invaluable facts and insights that can significantly enhance my life.

...I'd like to learn Torah with incredible clarity. To me, that means fully comprehending the nuances of the subject matter to such an extent that I can also readily apply it to my day-to-day life and even use it to help others.

...I'd like to abolish ALL of the media. I mean ALL of it. I'm curious what the lack of exposure to murders, catastrophes, gossip, traffic, corruption, oil cartels, profanity, steroids, gas prices, junk bonds, euthanasia, rap music, 0-percent financing, immorality, unemployment, the UN, focus groups, newfound diseases, drug lords, Blacktooths/Blackberries, movies, talk radio, bad breath, taxes, discrimination, George Steinbrenner, athlete's foot, and insurance commercials will do for my soul. I think I know the answer to that.

... I'd like to eliminate every clock in the universe. Must we constantly be held prisoner by time?

...I'd like to be unencumbered so I can really bond with my kids and my grandchildren.

...I'd like to see every single one of G-d's creations (that includes people, plants, emotions, and mangos) as just that — inventions of the Divine. I have a feeling that seven days of this brand of sacred immersion just might change me forever.

...I'd like to have enough money to experience what it's like to make a difference in the lives of a poor family.

...I'd like to finally understand music. That means figuring out what really makes a melody or a rhythm beautiful, how to compose, and why certain note combinations are harmonious while others sound like screeching chimps on a summer fast-day.

...I'd like to be rid of any vestige of fear that lurks deep inside me.

...I'd like to understand baby talk.

...I'd like to be stuck in traffic and not care.

...I'd like to meet Jeremiah...Daniel....Ezekiel...just to feel what it's like to be in their presence.

...I'd like to feel free to cry whenever I needed a really "good one."

...I'd like to see my father again, thank him the way I should have, respect him the way he deserved, and show him the love that I could never adequately express.

...I'd like to live in a world where finding fault would be punishable by law.

...I'd like to pretend that every day was Purim.

...I'd like to feel what it's like to have a sister.

...I'd like to have all my philosophical questions answered. Truthfully, there aren't that many. And I bet that once one or two of them are answered, the rest of them won't be questions any more.

...I'd like to remember all my dreams and understand them too.

...I'd like to be a Chassidic Rebbe or a Litvisher (of Lithuanian descent) Rosh Yeshivah or a Sephardic Leader and learn the true meaning of *"Serve the Lord with total joy."*

...I'd like to live in the times of the Temple — the First, Second, especially the Third. After that, I would write about it...and never have to wonder what to write about again.

But one week goes by very quickly.

And it does seem like there is a lot to do.

What are we waiting for?

One Final Word... or Two

A majority of the reflections you just read first appeared on the award-winning website of Aish Hatorah, **www.aish.com** I believe it critical to remind my readers that much has been written lately about the perils of Internet use. The potential dangers inherent in casual and unsupervised use of the Internet are great. At the same time, it must be realized that Internet use today is necessary for many individuals and businesses. And the capacity of Torah - based websites to dramatically impact the spirituality of millions of Jews cannot be ignored or underestimated. As with any other powerful tool, appropriate safeguards should always be implemented before use.

Y.S.